Meet and Three

MEET AND THREE
A Southern Gentleman's Philosophy on Connection and Life

Stafford Shurden

©2025 All Rights Reserved. No portion of this book may be reproduced, stored in a retrieval system, or transmitted in any form or by any means—electronic, mechanical, photocopy, recording, scanning, or other—except for brief quotations in critical reviews or articles without the prior permission of the author.

Published by Game Changer Publishing

Paperback ISBN: 978-1-968250-36-2
Hardcover ISBN: 978-1-968250-37-9
Digital ISBN: 978-1-968250-38-6

www.GameChangerPublishing.com

To my children, Mary Stafford and Anna Walton—
I'm sorry for all the nights I came in late from the farm,
the basketball games I missed, and the summer vacations we never took.
Thank you both for understanding. Daddy is very proud of
the young ladies you both have become.

To my wife, Leslie—
Thank you for standing by me through the hard times. Everyone knows
I outkicked my coverage with you. You have always had my back.

To Mom and Dad—
Thank you for perfect parenting. Thank you for rescuing me.

To Viola "Bolie" Shurden—
You gave me a love for food and for people
that I have built a life around.

And to the whole Shurden family—
Thank you for making me your own.

Read This First

Just to say thanks for buying and reading my book,
I would like to connect with you!

Scan the QR Code Here:

Stafford Shurden

Meet *and* Three

A Southern Gentleman's Philosophy
on Connection and Life

Foreword

Late last summer, my family went out for a lazy day on the Mississippi River, which runs along the edge of our land. Me, my wife, my girls, my cousin and his daughter, and their dog. I love the river. On its banks and in its fierce current is where and how we renew our ancient connections to the forces that put all of us here to begin with.

I can say now with confidence that we could feel the existential winter coming for our fragile home in the Mississippi Delta, where life is tied to the whims of every government in the world—most especially our own—and of the commodity markets that drive all human behavior which, if you look at them closely, expose the utter myth of free will. People are governed by fear and a desire to hold onto resources and invent moral frameworks for why they, and not some other person, should get those resources. Survival is the true god in the sky.

Even then, as harvest approached, prices were already falling, still tied to President Trump's tariff threats from his first term. This was before election day, when the price of cotton, corn, and soybeans went off a cliff, and when those same tariffs destroyed markets that had taken decades to build.

My cousin Thomas, a talented cotton farmer and the future of our family's operation, drove the boat. We listened to the Rolling Stones. The 115 Yamaha motored us to a sandbar where our little girls could play and swim and hunt for driftwood. He talked about the future. Credit markets would tighten, interest rates would rise, prices would fall, then rent prices would fall, then land value would fall, and with it the ability to borrow enough money to survive. A death spiral.

"That's gonna separate the men from the boys," he said.

The river shallowed as we got closer to the port of Rosedale. Low water makes it almost impossible for the barges to get beans down to New Orleans and doubles the shipping cost. The gauges measured seventeen feet as we slowed.

"What do you mean?" I asked.

I, of course, am a farmer in name only.

"Whether they're gonna make it or not," he said. "Whether they're gonna keep their land or have to sell it."

It hasn't been this bad since the 1980s, a farming crisis that did irreversible damage to the Mississippi Delta. Those lean years pushed out many old-line families, making way for institutional investors—from Prudential to Bill Gates—to quietly transform Mississippi once more into a colony for capital markets in big cities around the world, places that love to extract wealth from places like our home while also looking down their noses at us. The 1980s downturn even pushed out most of the famed Shurden family, whose headquarters were centered around Drew, Mississippi.

Their names started appearing in the local papers, and soon most of their empire had fallen out of their hands.

I met Stafford Shurden six years ago, and the first time we talked was out the windows of our trucks, parked tail to snout just off Highway 49 as it passes through Drew on the way to Parchman. This little piece of American dirt is his family's home place, which they once ruled. Now I think he's the last Shurden to farm it. He is both the end of something and the flickering promise that it doesn't have to end—not if each generation claws down into the dirt and refuses to be blown away. The American farmer is more vulnerable right now than at any moment in history—more than during the market-less wilderness of the Civil War, more than the twenty percent interest rates in the 1980s that gave birth to Willie Nelson and Bob Dylan's Farm Aid.

Stafford is the rare American standing in the breach of the coming agricultural apocalypse. As a farmer in the Delta, I can tell you how the future manifests itself in my anxiety and subconscious. I picture these black, churning fungal beasts loping across the land, like the aliens in that Tom Cruise movie. Stafford knows the falling price of beans and the loss of three quarters of our markets, and I don't think he even plants cotton anymore. He rents land his family once owned, but he refuses to quit. This is the stuff America should be built on.

He has bet his entire self on the belief that his town will survive through his farming, his politics, his restaurant, his duck gumbo festival, and his riding lawn mower Mardi Gras parade. In his cultish YouTube series about Southern gas station food—a kind, rollicking marriage of Anthony Bourdain's love of the common man and Dave Portnoy's pizza ratings—he bets his entire self on the belief that your town will survive, too. He's the very definition of a good ol' boy, and not in the Boss Hogg, Eastland, political-operator way, but in the way Willie Morris meant it. Stafford is absolutely the product of one of the most tribal, parochial corners of the American backcountry, yet he remains open to the new, wild possibilities of unknown horizons. He's a loving father and a loyal friend.

He's also country as shit.

This book is his story.

It is my fervent wish that you also read it as my story. And if you're from the South—especially the Mississippi Delta—I hope you read it as your story, too. If you're not from here and are just a fan of his television show, then take this as a rare document from deep inside a world that otherwise, you'd never be able to access as an outsider. It is a chronicle of home and a fight to hold home in your hands, to define it, to feel safe in it, to pass it along to your children.

Down here, we are all hunkered down against the coming existential winter, determined to survive, to protect our home, writ small, and our home, writ large. The poetry and the prose of our Delta land. Prices are falling, interest rates are rising, markets are shrinking and turning to dust, and all of this damage was done to Mississippi not by a foreign power, not by God or His weather, not by China, which farms cotton with slave labor, not by India, which pays a fraction of what we pay, but by ourselves. That's the conundrum of Mississippi—a place fighting for its life, always, against many outside forces, but mostly always against itself. We've fought against Democrats with environmental regulations written by people who've never put a seed in the dirt. And we've fought against Republicans, whose actions right now suggest a desire to end the American farmer—

and the fragile American farming town. Towns like Drew, Shelby, and Bentonia. It's frustrating to get it from both sides, but we are born fighters. People like Stafford are beacons that suggest those fights are winnable, that they are worth winning.

It is a chronicle of a past, yes, but also a prayer for the future.

—Wright Thompson

Preface: The Tie That Binds

The hum of the tires on my truck shifts from the steady drone of Highway 49 to a crunching sound as I turn west onto the gravel of Fitzhugh Road. Shurden Farms is just a mile down, but already I can see the stark difference between today and yesterday. Rain fell this morning, and now both the corn and soybeans glisten with a deeper green, framed by a setting sun casting hues of orange and gold across the fields. Most of the rain clouds have drifted east, leaving a picturesque scene in their wake.

It's funny how water from the heavens can transform things. A single drop of rain, mingling with millions—or trillions—of others, brings life-giving sustenance to the crops. The cooler temperatures are a welcome respite from the long, hot days of late June in Mississippi. I've largely done my job: we chose great varieties, invested in necessary fertilizers, planted on time, and kept the farm free of noxious weeds. You control what you can and pray for what you can't.

Today is a moment of grace. That's what I've always loved about farming: you do your part, and then you surrender. In the end, you obey something larger than your own ambition. That's the nature of the job. Obedience—not just discipline, but surrender to the process. It's about connection.

June also brings my birthday. I'll be fifty-one in a few days. This will be my twenty-ninth crop, not counting the years I was helping on the farm when I was ten or twelve. Things were harder then. Simpler, too. I grew up on a cotton farm, but now we plant soybeans, corn, rice, and occasionally winter wheat and grain sorghum. Tractors have air conditioning now, GPS guidance, and yield maps—but the hands on the wheel still need calluses.

Farmers just know things. You don't learn it in a book—you earn it in dirt. Years of watching crops respond to care and chaos have taught me how to read the land, and read people too. Farming trained me for everything I've ever done: running for office, raising kids, launching a business. It's all about timing, patience, and knowing when to act. You are connected: to the soil, to your family, to your neighbors. And when the food you grow hits a barge on the river, you're connected to the whole world. You make decisions and live with the outcome. You show up, again and again, for yourself, but also for others.

There would be no food service without farmers—we're the original entrepreneurs. But the real gift of farming isn't the harvest. It's the mindset. We live in obedience to seasons, to storms, to truths that don't bend just because we want them to. And that mindset has shaped how I've run every part of my life—from a Delta courtroom to a small-town restaurant that somehow found its way onto the *Best of Mississippi* list.

As I drive across the farm today, I see the fruit of that connection. The crops are growing, and so is something else—an idea, a reflection. My restaurant, Stafford's Market, is two decades old now. After years of challenges, it's found its rhythm and connection to the community. But it's more than just a restaurant. It's a place where people feel seen. Where strangers turn into friends over chicken and cornbread.

I've worn a lot of hats: husband, father, son, farmer, judge, restaurateur, and now, somehow, an influencer. It's a strange collection of titles, and on the surface, they don't seem to fit together. But one thing binds them all: connection.

That's the gift I've been given. It's not cooking or farming or speaking on a stage. It's the ability to connect with people. To see them. To understand what they need, even when they don't say it out loud. Whether I'm handing a plate across a counter or filming a gas station food review out of the back of my truck, I'm doing the same thing: building bridges. That's what food does best. That's what I try to do with my life.

Food is the tie that binds. It's more than sustenance; it's sacred. Farming and breaking bread are biblical acts, rooted in tradition and stitched with grace. Food crosses lines of race, class, and geography. It's a shared language, one that connects us in a way nothing else can.

In the South, we have the "meat and three"—a tradition older than most of the buildings it's served in. Some say it came from post-church meals eaten on the ground under oak trees. Others trace it to the country diners that fed hardworking men something hot and hearty. Either way, it's more than a plate—it's a philosophy. As a play on words, for me, it has been *meet* and three.

Meet and three is about balance. About making the most of what you've got. It's about abundance without waste, hospitality without pretense. And for me, it's a metaphor that touches everything I do. From Mammy's kitchen, to the back room of a gas station in Arkansas, to the counter at Stafford's Market—it's the one thread that's never frayed.

Food is a story. Food is my story. But more than that, food is how I connect. It's how I obey the calling I've been given. It's how I remind people that they matter. And maybe—if we do it right—it's how we tie it all together: faith, family, farming, and food, the connector.

Table of Contents

Part I: Where I Come From 1

    Chapter 1: The Greatest Gift 3

    Chapter 2: Blue-Collar Palate 7

    Chapter 3: Choppin' Cotton 13

    Chapter 4: The Grandma Rule 17

    Chapter 5: Johnson Grass and Catfish 21

    Chapter 6: Mississippi Delta Camping 25

    Chapter 7: Real Farming... 29

    Chapter 8: Bubbaisms... 35

    Chapter 9: Father Figures 41

    Chapter 10: Go West, Young Man 49

    Chapter 11: College Knowledge 55

    Chapter 12: Back to the Delta 59

Part II: Try, Fail, Learn 63

    Chapter 13: Straw Boss... 65

    Chapter 14: My Turn 69

    Chapter 15: First Year Luck.. 73

    Chapter 16: The Bored Farmer.. 77

    Chapter 17: Shurden Construction Co 81

    Chapter 18: Main Street Deli & Gifts... 83

    Chapter 19: The School of Hard Knocks....................................... 87

    Chapter 20: Judge Stafford Shurden 91

    Chapter 21: Autopilot.. 97

Part III: Setting the Table 101

    Chapter 22: 1933 103

    Chapter 23: "A Man Ain't Nothing if He Ain't Got Land" 111

    Chapter 24: Restaurant Makeover 115

    Chapter 25: A Social World 119

    Chapter 26: 2020 125

    Chapter 27: Summer Rain 131

    Chapter 28: Replanting and Championships 135

    Chapter 29: Bootcamp 139

    Chapter 30: The Line Doesn't Hold Itself 143

Part IV: Lessons, Legacy, Mindset 147

    Chapter 31: A New Vision—The Grandma Rule 149

    Chapter 32: Worst to First 155

    Chapter 33: Ancestors or Ghosts 159

    Chapter 34: The Meet and Three Philosophy 163

    Chapter 35: The Road Home 167

    Chapter 36: What It All Comes Down To 171

Appendix: On the Road Again: Gas Station Tailgate Review 173

PART I

Where I Come From

CHAPTER 1

The Greatest Gift

I don't know where I was born. That detail remains a mystery to me. My birth certificate says Drew, Mississippi, but I don't believe that to be inaccurate—perhaps a way to hide the truth. I'm mostly sure of my birthdate, June 30, 1973, though even that carries a shadow of uncertainty. I was born to people who, for reasons I'll never fully understand, didn't want me. Thankfully, in August of that same year, I came home to Drew, cradled in the arms of my new and proud parents, Andrew Walton "Bubba" Shurden and Ann Dow Shurden.

Bubba was a young cotton farmer. He stood tall, with jet-black hair and piercing blue eyes. His life was a balancing act between farming and military service in his early years, but eventually, he chose to dedicate himself fully to the land. Farming was in his blood—he was the son of Reg Shurden, who was the son of George Shurden, each generation of Shurden men tied to the Mississippi Delta's soil. Dad's military discipline sharpened his focus, making him a natural at managing the demands of farming. He was also remarkably even-tempered. I can remember him getting angry, maybe once. He was measured and fair. He passed away from cancer in 2006 at the young age of sixty-three.

My mom, Ann Dow, was—in my mind—a Greenwood debutante. She was a stunning blonde, and at eighty-two, she remains beautiful and blonde to this day. Raised by her mother, Lucille, a schoolteacher, she grew up strong and resilient. Her father, Edgar, passed away at just forty-five while showing his prized bulldog—it was the best day of his life, and it was his last. I carry his name as my middle name, a small but meaningful connection to the man I never knew. Lucille moved to Germany and taught English after Edgar died. When she returned, she taught reading to illiterate adults. She was prim and proper and would say things like, "Son, you are butchering the King's English," if I used *ain't* in a sentence. She lived another fifty-six years without Edgar, passing away at 101. She never learned to cook, but she would be ever proud of me for writing. Mom, like her mother, has always been a cheerleader and a teacher, loving and encouraging. She provided the perfect counterbalance to my dad's more disciplined parenting style. Together, they struck a harmony that shaped me in the best possible way.

When my parents struggled to have children of their own, they turned to adoption. The process was anything but quick. Eventually, they were matched with me. A few tests stood between them and their dream of becoming parents, and they passed them all—well, almost all of them.

One test involved ensuring their home had access to clean water. At the time, my parents lived in a little white house out in the country, drawing water from an old well. The test failed. The man conducting it returned for another round, and again, it failed. On his third visit, the water miraculously passed. Years later, my parents told me the truth: that kind man had stopped by his own house, filled the container with his own water, and submitted it on their behalf, ensuring I could finally come home. It's a gesture that brings tears to my eyes even as I type this. A small miracle that changed the course of my life just as it began.

Being adopted is hard to put into words. On one hand, at the most vulnerable moment of my life, the people who should have cared for me the most simply didn't. On the other hand, two strangers—Bubba and Ann Dow—*chose* me. They took me in, made me theirs, and surrounded me with a love so complete it defied words. It's a strange dichotomy: a sense of belonging and not belonging, all at once. Abandonment tempered by absolute, unconditional love.

For me, this duality has shaped my understanding of family. I know how precious it is to be loved, to be fed, to be cared for. I also know how close I came to not having any of that. To this day, it remains the greatest gift I've ever been given. It's a debt I can never fully repay—but I try every single day.

CHAPTER 2

Blue-Collar Palate

A few months ago, I was a guest on a friend's podcast. One of the hosts introduced me as "Judge Stafford Shurden, the man with the blue-collar palate."

I told him right then and there I was stealing that line—and I meant it. It just hit right because it felt honest. It felt like *me*.

I like to think of myself as a man's man, the way my dad was.

I was raised around people who believed in hard work, straight talk, and sitting down to a plate of food that didn't need translating. Meals weren't built to impress you—they were built to feed you: body and soul.

I love that kind of food. The kind that's a little greasy, a little messy, a little too much—but in all the right ways. Food that isn't worried about being photographed, only about being eaten. That food is the story of my youth, and over time, it's become something more: a teaching tool. It's the easiest way I know to open a door, break down a barrier, and find common ground with a stranger.

Turns out, a plate of fried chicken will tear down a wall faster than any five-star meal ever could.

Don't get me wrong—I love both. I've sat at white tablecloths and eaten things with names I couldn't pronounce, and I'm grateful for every bite. But there's something about fried chicken... or a burger so juicy it runs down your arms... or a pot of red beans and rice that's been on the stove all day... that speaks a different kind of language. It's comfortable. It's *home*. And I think the world needs more of that right now.

When you sit down with someone over a plate of food like that, you're not sizing each other up. You're not worried about titles, or bank accounts, or which side of town you came from. You're just two people, eating. And in a world that seems hell-bent on reminding us how different we are, a plate of good, honest food can remind us how much we still have in common.

Maybe that's why I've always felt drawn to it—the fried chicken joints, the barbecue shacks, the gas station griddles hidden out on some forgotten highway. It's not just about the taste, although the taste is damn sure worth the trip. It's about the feeling that in this messed-up world, there is a place you belong, with no reservations required.

That sense of belonging—that bone-deep craving for home, even when you don't quite know where home is—has always been a part of my story. Long before I understood it fully, I was living it, bite by bite.

And a lot of that story leads back to the people who gave me their name, their table, and their way of life: the Shurden family.

*****

Granddaddy Reg, born in 1917, was the youngest son of Mr. and Mrs. George Shurden. George had made his way to Mississippi from Georgia and St. Augustine, Florida, where his father had arrived from Ireland on a cattle boat. George settled in Maben, Mississippi, and followed in his father's footsteps—trading mules and farming a few acres of cotton. He and Grandma Shurden had eighteen children: ten boys and eight girls.

Uncle Otha once wrote that the Shurden family grew up in Maben, "rich in the things that made life important," though they had to work hard to earn a living. They always had food on the table, and food was central to their lives. Fruit trees and sorghum molasses meant there were always sweets. George knew how to fatten a hog and grow enough corn to last through the winter. Grandma Shurden tended a massive garden filled with beans, cabbages, greens, and tomatoes. There was enough to ensure every meal had a meat and three, even though she rarely ate meat herself.

In 1921, when Granddaddy Reg was four, the family moved by train to Drew, Mississippi. It was the first time Reg and Otha had ever seen a train—and it scared them. They made their way to nearby Mathiston, loading everything they owned—including the milk cow—onto that train, taking a leap of faith into the still-developing frontier of the Delta. Some of the older brothers, like Bob, were already in Drew, farming cotton and finding success. Bob convinced their father, George, that the Delta held more promise, so the rest of the family followed.

Being the youngest, Granddaddy Reg outlived most of his brothers, but not by much. He died in 1979, and Uncle Otha, the last of the ten brothers, passed in 1986. I suppose I knew Otha best of all the brothers, as my dad—Bubba, his nephew—farmed all of Otha's land. Otha's presence was larger than life, and his reputation matched.

A book could be written about my grandfather and his brothers. Most started as sharecroppers and eventually owned land, pulling themselves from abject poverty into the upper middle class in a single generation. I don't think any of them graduated from college, and a few didn't finish high school. They worked hard, endured tough years, and found their way. As far as anyone knows, they were all honest men—men who built their lives on trust and perseverance.

There are stories worth telling. Uncle Clint once drove and protected Willie Reed, an 18-year-old terrified for his life, so he could testify against murderers at the Emmett Till trial. Clint waited until the testimony was done, then brought him back to Drew. Willie later connected with Medgar Evers and fled to Chicago. Uncle Elbert, Bob's son, was a WWII hero. When he passed, the mayor of Drew ordered every flag in town to be flown at half-staff. Elbert also donated the "Shurden Bell" to the town. It sits in the park across from my restaurant, with my Granddaddy Reg's name etched in brass alongside his brothers and sisters.

Granddaddy Reg once had a farm worker die in a car crash. He paid for the man's funeral and gave his best suit for the man to be buried in. He also gave the widow money, pressing it into her hand with one instruction: "Don't spend this on anything but college for that little boy. It's his only way out."

Years later, I was standing in my restaurant when a well-dressed Black man walked through the door, asking for my dad. "I'm sorry," I told him. "He's passed."

The man reached out his hand and said, "I just wanted to shake the hand of someone in this family. That act of kindness changed my life."

I had never heard that story before. Here I was, a grown man, and the acts of my grandfather, who had been gone for thirty years, were still coming to light.

It was emotional for both of us. He was living proof of what quiet generosity could do—the kind that doesn't come with strings attached or expectations of praise. It was also a stark reminder of the kind of heritage I was adopted into: a legacy built on doing the right thing, even when the world wasn't watching.

And then there was Otha—the brother whose name carried weight. He drank scotch with LBJ and Lady Bird at the president's ranch in Texas, made oil deals with D. A. Biglane and Bunker Hunt, and co-wrote parts of the 1969 Farm Bill with Senator James "Big Jim" Eastland. Otha's larger-than-life presence had a profound impact on my dad, Bubba Shurden, and in turn, on me. It made me think bigger. Otha had no fear.

Dad started with very little as well, farming out of the Ford Thunderbird he bought in college. He couldn't find land in Drew, so Otha helped him secure a farm in Flora, Mississippi, where he farmed for a few years before returning to Drew.

Dad told me he went bankrupt in 1969—not legally, but in spirit. He couldn't pay back both his farm loan (it was called a *furnish* back then because the seed dealer would literally furnish the things needed to make a crop) and the rent he owed. His landlords carried him for a year so he could pay back the bank. Dad said he sat on the floor and cried, swearing he'd never be broke again.

He never was.

He had a good crop the next year, paid his landlords back with two years' rent, and started signing his name with a dollar sign for the "S" in Shurden. $hurden. The man manifested his destiny. He also had no fear—even when he knew he was dying.

I can't forget the Shurden girls' impact on farming. My sister's son, John William Madison, wants to farm and now works with me. My cousin Jimmy Haney is one of the most successful farmers in Mississippi, although he would just as soon no one knew it.

With that said, of all the descendants of the ten Shurden brothers, I will be the last with the Shurden name to farm the fertile land of the Mississippi Delta. It's a privilege, but it's also heavy. To the family that took me in and made me their own, I owe a debt to carry this tradition forward as long as I can. It is a connection I can never repay.

My friend Wright Thompson once told me, "You can either be an ancestor or a ghost." You can tether your family's history together—or let it drag you down by being chained to it. It's hard to know which you're doing sometimes, but I feel the presence of my ancestors. And I think that's a good thing.

Faith, family, farming, and food.

That is the Shurden legacy.

That is the tie that binds.

CHAPTER 3

Choppin' Cotton

The summer of 1983 was the year I turned ten, and I adored my dad. In our house, we all slept with the doors open. At night, I could hear my dad snoring. My mom will probably be mortified that I'm writing this, but I could hear her snoring too! More importantly, I could hear my dad when he got up to go to work. The rustle of his boots on the floor and the creak of the saloon doors in my parents' bathroom was my alarm clock. I'd leap out of bed, throw on my "work clothes," slap on a ball cap, and tag along to the farm. That was our routine, day in and day out.

Back then, planting cotton was an art. My dad would trail the planters all day, checking to make sure those tiny seeds were placed just right—deep enough to reach the moisture, but not so deep that a rainstorm would bury them beyond hope.

One day, we'd walked about half a mile from the truck—a 1983 Chevy El Camino—when he turned to me and said, "Go get the truck."

"But Daddy, I don't know how to drive," I replied, wide-eyed.

"You'll figure it out," he said, as if it were the simplest thing in the world. And it was.

So, I did what I was told. I trekked back to the truck, climbed in, and drove it over. It wasn't graceful, but I made it. Later, I learned to drive a stick shift in much the same way. That "you'll figure it out" mantra became the cornerstone of how I was raised. And looking back, it was the best kind of childhood.

Rainy days on the farm meant time in the shop, fixing equipment, and preparing for when the fields dried out. On those mornings, I'd sleep in a little, then hop on my Honda 110 three-wheeler and ride up to the shop—just to be where my dad was.

The shop was where I first met Billy Williams, our bookkeeper. Mr. Billy was a character—a married man with no kids who dressed to impress: rhinestone jewelry, fancy clothes, you name it. Every Christmas, he'd give me silver dollars. I still have some of them. Mr. Billy also owned the gas station next door, which doubled as a men's clothing store. You could even rent a tux there, in the gas station. And on Mondays, a barber named Tiny would cut hair in the back. It was the kind of place that could only exist in Drew, Mississippi, and it was awesome.

Mr. Billy had a '57 Cadillac Eldorado—the one with the fins. When I was old enough, I would drive it in the Christmas parades. I even drove Miss Delta State once. She ended up marrying a guy from Drew.

Mr. Billy also had an amazing yard that he called "The Rebel Terrace" because he was a huge Archie fan—the legendary quarterback who played for the University of Mississippi in the late 1960s and early 1970s. That admiration made him an Ole Miss Rebel fan, even though he never attended college there.

The yard was beautiful, filled with tropical plants that should never have survived Mississippi winters. I was always amazed by the banana tree.

Mr. Billy would throw huge parties on The Rebel Terrace. One was called Oktoberfest. Otha was there, along with Senator Eastland and, I'm sure, more than one governor. Uncle Otha had a pet monkey, and I've heard tales about that monkey getting drunk at one of those parties. Mr. Billy said the monkey was having a good time, but was hungover the next day and just lay at the bottom of his cage.

On one of those rainy shop days, Mr. Billy, with all his rhinestone jewelry on, offered me a job pumping gas for a dollar an hour. A dollar an hour! That night, I asked my dad what he thought.

"You want to work?" he asked.

The very next day, instead of pumping gas—or maybe even carrying hors d'oeuvres around a fancy party—I found myself across the road from our house, chopping cotton for that same dollar an hour. I got so sunburned out there, I can still feel it. I probably wasn't worth the dollar they paid me, and I didn't last long. Later, I graduated to picking up chunks—clearing land for center pivots by gathering pieces of wood too small for the tractors and tossing them into a fire. In July. In Mississippi.

Once again, I wasn't worth the dollar an hour.

The best part of those days wasn't the work; it was lunch at Mrs. Sullivan's. Her place was an old gas station turned restaurant, where every day she served a meat and three, along with fried pies and the best barbecue I've ever had. She had a brick pit built into the wall and a cutting block worn so deeply from years of chopping barbecue that it resembled a bowl. I'm pretty sure every sandwich she made had a little bit of that chopping block in it. It didn't matter—it was good. I can taste it now.

Sitting in her restaurant with all the old farmers gave me a sense of connection. Farming always came with food, and food always came with fellowship. Mrs. Sullivan's has been gone for years, but today at Stafford's Market, we have a big table where the farmers sit to eat our meat and three. It's a tribute to those men I ate with as a kid—and to Mrs. Sullivan, who fed us. What I received at her table was so much more than just food.

CHAPTER 4

The Grandma Rule

The first tractor I learned to drive was a small 284 International with a mower attached. This was long before the era of large zero-turns, and our four-acre yard required something substantial. Dad's farm manager, Thomas Hall, gave me a few verbal instructions and turned me loose. I didn't get paid for mowing the lawn—it was just a chore.

When I finished with our yard, I would drive the little tractor about two miles down the road and across Highway 49 to my grandmother's house to mow her yard. Her name was Viola Jones Shurden. For some reason, my grandfather—Granddaddy Reg—called her "Bolie." I heard someone say that her sister called her that once, and it stuck. When my Aunt Debra was born, she had trouble saying "Momma," and it came out "Mammy." That's how things happen in the South. A name gets stuck in a gear and never quite shakes out.

Though "Mammy" might not pass the tests of today's world, to me, it's a name steeped in memories of endless, unyielding love. It's a word that feels like home, heavy with the warmth of her kitchen and the softness of her presence. Mammy was one of the kindest, most genuine souls I've ever known. Everyone in Drew knew her by that name. Even my friends, neighbors, and people who didn't know her well called her Mammy. It wasn't just what we called her; it was who she was—a title that carried the weight of her sweetness and the boundless love she gave to everyone lucky enough to sit at her table.

She and Granddaddy Reg slept in separate queen beds in their room. Once, someone asked her, "How'd y'all end up having five kids then?" and she grinned and said, "Reg had a path cut across there." That was Mammy—always a bit playful, never too serious, and never short on a good line.

When I was just a little kid, I would cry until Granddaddy Reg came to get me. I'd stay up late with them and watch Johnny Carson, or I'd talk Granddaddy into sleeping with me in his Airstream camper in the yard. He died in 1979 at the age of sixty-two. I was six.

When I went to mow Mammy's yard, I learned that my payment would come in the form of food. I never asked for it, but I soon figured out that if I started mowing around ten in the morning, Mammy would start cooking. I made a point to mow right up by the house so she could hear the little tractor.

Chicken and dumplings were my favorite, and she made a heavy, creamy dumpling. The chicken wasn't even that important. She made drop-style cathead biscuits, too. A lot of days, she would fry the little drumstick section from a chicken wing just for me. She always kept those in the fridge. Sometimes she'd cook bigger pieces in her old black iron skillet, frying them up to a dark, brassy-gold color. She also made the best cornbread shaped like little ears of corn. She kept her bread in a mailbox that sat on the counter beside a cake dish that always held some kind of homemade cake. She almost always had ambrosia—a Southern salad with pineapple and cherry—that we would all spoon onto our cake. Her tea was as sweet as those desserts, but not as sweet as she was.

On Christmas Eve, all her kids and their kids would gather at her house to eat her cooking. Tired of turkey, at some point, the men started doing prime rib, and that eventually turned into whole filet mignon. Now, the tradition continues at my house—the same one I grew up in with the four-acre yard. There are usually about thirty-five of us on Christmas Eve. All descendants, or married to descendants, of Mammy. It's the closest thing we have to a family reunion. It's beautiful—full of great food and love. I think she would be proud that we still do it.

When Mammy passed away, they asked if there was anything of hers I might want. I chose that cast-iron skillet—the one in which she made the little cornbread sticks.

Mammy's love language toward me was food. She's a huge influence on how I see food and on the kind of food we serve in our restaurant. Our restaurant culture of food and connection is *her*. We call it the "Grandma Rule." I could say we cook country cooking or soul food, but what we really cook is the kind of food our grandmothers made for us. And we treat every customer as if they were one of our grandmothers in disguise. One of my biggest regrets is naming the restaurant after me and not her.

That sweetest of sweethearts—the woman who sparked my lifelong love of feeding people—died on Valentine's Day in 1998. Somehow, it feels right that her heart would stop on the day we celebrate love. But she's still here—in the way we cook and connect with people, in the memory of a warm kitchen and that special skillet, and in the traditions that bind us all together at the table.

Faith, family, farming, and food.

CHAPTER 5

Johnson Grass and Catfish

A few years after I'd worn out my trusty Honda 110 three-wheeler, my dad bought me a brand-new Honda four-wheeler. My mom hated it. She called it the "death machine," which still makes me laugh every time I think about it. She wasn't entirely wrong, though—I did break my arm on that old four-wheeler when I ran it straight into a massive crepe myrtle in our yard. I remember my cousin, Dallas, crying because he thought I'd killed myself in the carnage of that old bush.

Dad, always the diplomat, smoothed things over by calling the four-wheeler "farm equipment." To back it up, we outfitted it with a three-row sprayer, and I got a promotion: spraying Johnson grass. It was a big step up from tossing chunks of wood into a fire. I loved it. Straddling mile-long rows of cotton on my four-wheeler, hunting down Johnson grass, and spraying it felt like a mission. The herbicide we used turned the grass purple before it dried out to a crispy brown, and I took pride in spotting the enemy and taking it down.

One of the farms we worked was called Blue Lake, way over in Tallahatchie County. I'd drive my four-wheeler all the way out there to spray grass. Lunchtime at Blue Lake meant a trip to Robinson's Grocery, a true Mississippi gem. It was a one-stop shop that sold gas, cold-cut sandwiches, and firearms. My dad had a farm charge account there, so all the workers—big, strong, African-American men—and me, this scrawny white kid, would sit under the shade trees, eating bologna sandwiches and stage plank cookies.

On rare days, my dad would join us. His lunch was a Twinkie wrapped in bologna. He said that when he was young, his dad would give him lunch money—just enough for a Coke, two slices of bread, and a slice of bologna. It wasn't enough for a Twinkie unless he skipped the bread. At some point, he had the epiphany to wrap the Twinkie with the bologna, and that crazy combination was born. To this day, I can't bring myself to try it, but he ate it like it was a delicacy.

Rainy days were no longer shop days for me—I'd caught the fishing bug. The four-wheeler opened up new horizons, and my parents were cool enough to let me roam. I'd disappear for hours, fishing at Long Lake or driving out to a place called the Lost Forty, owned by Mr. Red Parker. It was his son, Mike, who married the beauty queen, Pam—Miss Delta State. Mr. Red was a catfish farmer and always let me fish his ponds. Let me tell you, dear reader, that was the kind of fishing dreams are made of. You couldn't lose.

My buddy, Walt Cummins, and I would catch a mess of fish, ride back to his house on the four-wheeler, and clean them. His momma would fry them up right there for us. Those were some of the best meals I've ever had—not just because of the fish, but because of the friendship and freedom that came with those adventures.

At that age, I didn't care a thing about sports. I had two great loves: farming and the outdoors. If I wasn't in a field spraying Johnson grass or helping out on the farm, I was wetting a hook or taking my little 20-gauge A-5 Browning shotgun out to hunt. That was my life back then, and I couldn't have been happier. I was like the Indiana Jones of the Delta—always looking for adventure and the treasure of bringing something home to cook and eat, and always with friends.

CHAPTER 6

Mississippi Delta Camping

Once I had my freedom in the form of a four-wheeler, it seemed the countryside of the Mississippi Delta became my oyster. Every day brought new discoveries—new people to fish with, and new friends who also had four-wheelers. Most of my friends were older: Trey, John, Dean, Rusty, and Donnie (who were brothers), Wilton, Travis, and Sam. I'll dispense with last names to protect them from any possible prosecution.

Boys become men by pushing the envelope of what's acceptable in society, and while I have a pretty squeaky-clean reputation, I did test a few boundaries in my youth. It seemed almost encouraged. I'm part of Generation X, also known as the latchkey kids. At fourteen, I had a key to our house and could come and go as I pleased. I didn't have a cell phone and would often be gone for hours—or even days—when we went "camping." As long as I was back home for church on Sundays, my mom was cool with it. That was a lot of trust in retrospect. Thanks, Mom.

I started camping early in life by asking for a tent for Christmas and pitching it in our backyard. I was a literal Boy Scout, so I'd dig a hole and place rocks around it to make a little fire pit. A friend and I would cook in the coals, something we called a "hobo." (I haven't checked, but I imagine that's one of those politically incorrect terms now.) It was seasoned hamburger meat with onions and bell peppers, wrapped in aluminum foil, and cooked right in the fire. We ate like explorers—or so we thought. After eating, I'd cover the coals so they'd stay hot. In the morning, I'd uncover them and cook eggs with a little kit my dad had from his army days. If the coals were still hot enough, I'd even fry some bacon.

When I got a little older, my friends and I would ride our four-wheelers down to Bear Hollow, behind Rusty and Donnie's house, and camp. This was a little different. There was beer. How it was procured, I do not know—but there was always a hidden case of hot beer around Bear Hollow. For whatever reason, I never cared for that part. I didn't like the taste, and I didn't understand the appeal. I never drank in high school and didn't start until I was of legal drinking age. It just didn't suit me.

It didn't matter. My friends drank the beer, and we'd ride our four-wheelers all night, finding mudholes and ditches to jump. It was a blast. From my perspective, I had just as much fun, without the beer and without the headache.

Still, I managed to find trouble. There were always some kind of explosives: fireworks, for sure, but most of us also had guns. Writing this now, in today's world, it seems crazy that we were young teenagers with beer, fireworks, and guns, and no supervision. Occasionally, I'd sneak some ditching dynamite out of Dad's farm shop. It was used to blow up beaver dams on the farm, but we just liked blowing up random stuff. We would shoot bottle rockets and Roman candles at each other, our four-wheelers passing in the dark like knights on horseback. We'd build huge fires with the pallets that delivered seed to the farm. Someone always threw firecrackers into the fire, sending coals flying across the campsite and burning holes in our tents.

One night, Sam got the bright idea that we should ride around and throw firecrackers at houses. He was the oldest and had a green Ford truck. It was great fun—until it wasn't. We didn't even consider how terrible an idea it was. There were a lot of Vietnam vets around, and we had no idea what PTSD was back then. One of the houses belonged to a lady who worked with Sam's mom. Needless to say, she recognized his truck. When I got home, my parents already knew.

They were waiting with their trap set. "So, how was camping? Anything interesting happen?" Thank goodness I was at least smart enough not to lie. I spilled my guts, though I probably blamed most of the firecracker incident on Sam. After all, it was his truck, and he chose the houses, including the one with the lady he knew.

We were like a small army. A battalion of boys to be feared, traversing the countryside of Sunflower County, creating chaos and looking for trouble. I've heard that God takes care of fools. We were definitely fools—but I remember those times with such fondness. The miracle is that none of our tribe ever got seriously injured in any of those camping sessions. We'd hear about kids getting killed on ATVs in other places, but we somehow escaped, remarkably unscathed—both in reputation and in body.

There were bonding moments too. Most mornings, everyone but me would be hungover. I'd get up as if I were in my own backyard and cook breakfast—bacon and eggs in the coals, using that same little pan of my dad's. We'd sit on the pallets we hadn't gotten around to burning and just talk. We were learning—how to tell stories, how to understand each other, and most of all, how to understand ourselves. All that pent-up male energy burned out from a night of chaos, we became real friends, sitting around that fire, eating bacon and eggs.

CHAPTER 7

Real Farming

It didn't take long for the cotton to outgrow what my little four-wheeler could handle in the rows. By June of that same year, I was driving an old John Deere 4630 with an eight-row spray boom. I had graduated to the big leagues, spraying cotton from the seat of a full-size tractor until the cotton was "laid by."

"Laying by" meant the cotton's leaves had fully shaded the ground, preventing new weeds from getting enough sunlight to grow. This typically happened around the Fourth of July, shortly before the first cotton blooms appeared. In the old days, this marked a lull in the workload until harvest season. Sharecroppers would often use this time to focus on their gardens.

By the 1980s, however, we had moved far from the sharecropping system and toward a more high-maintenance farming model, with irrigation and new crops like soybeans and rice that demanded constant attention late into the growing season.

Dad's farm manager, Thomas Hall, would spend July preparing the cotton pickers for harvest, checking every part of the machine to avoid costly breakdowns. The other farm manager, John Henry Johnson, worked on laying out the gated pipe to irrigate the cotton. As for me, I was assigned to J. D. Williams to help check on the rice.

Rice was still a relatively new crop on our farm and required obsessive, daily care. It wasn't glamorous work—trudging through water and mud, acre after acre, day after day. But JD made it look easy. The guy was a machine: lean, athletic, like he'd been carved out of the very gumbo mud we were walking through. His long legs and confident stride made it seem like he should be suiting up for the NFL, not slogging through rice fields.

For six weeks that summer, I tried to keep up with JD, a shovel slung over my shoulder like I knew what I was doing. Spoiler: I didn't. I never complained out loud, but I might as well have been a rock tied to his ankle. My short legs and soft edges were no match for his pace. JD moved through the mud like it was second nature; I flailed through it like a drowning man.

The only real relief came at lunchtime. Mrs. Sullivan's place was the oasis in my swampy world. Every day, we got an hour to recover, and I counted down the seconds until I could collapse at her table. Wednesdays were the best: fried chicken day. Unlike me, it wasn't soggy. It was crispy perfection.

JD would drop me off and vanish, probably enjoying his hour of peace without having to drag me along. Then, like clockwork, he'd return—cool, unbothered, and ready to dive back in. No judgment, no commentary. Just another day for him. For me, it was survival. I wasn't a rising star or a farm kid learning the ropes. I was just another grunt in the mud, trying to keep up with a man who seemed born for it.

I must have done okay, because the next summer, I graduated to driving a tractor to plow cotton. That same year, I turned fifteen and got my driver's license. Dad let me drive myself to the tractor each morning and to lunch afterward. It felt like a rite of passage. I was driving with the big guys now—more freedom than ever. I felt like a big dog, and I absolutely loved it.

I loved plowing cotton. I just remember the satisfaction of doing that job. I loved having a cab with air conditioning and a radio! Nobody farms that way anymore—it's all minimum-till or no-till now—but there was something beautiful about the clean, straight lines left behind after a good plowing. I wasn't a bad driver, either. Well, mostly.

One Saturday, I learned the hard way that "mostly" just doesn't cut it. I was driving back to park the tractor, feeling good—maybe a little too good—and definitely going too fast. It's hard to explain how twenty miles an hour on a tractor can feel reckless, but trust me, it was. The thing had a 200-gallon tank mounted on the front that acted as a stabilizer when it was full of water and chemicals. But, it being the end of the day, I'd done the responsible thing and timed it perfectly so the tank was empty. Great for efficiency. Terrible for physics.

I hit a bump. Not a big one—just enough to send the front end floating up like a Mississippi Delta dragonfly. Suddenly, I wasn't steering anymore. I was just along for the ride. Helpless. The tractor drifted sideways, and that John Deere cultivator—my trusty sidekick—met its fate against a tree. "Met its fate" is putting it mildly. I mangled that cultivator. Twisted steel and broken pride. It was a wreck. I managed to limp the tractor back to the lot, where the crew was already waiting. They didn't even try to hide their amusement. By the time I parked, they were laughing outright. Mr. Thomas, who normally had plenty to say, was uncommonly quiet. He walked up, took one long look at the damage, and said, "I don't have anything to say. I'm just gonna let you tell your dad about this."

Terror. Pure, uncut terror. That's what I felt driving home. When I got there, I sat down at the kitchen table, tears welling up as I spilled the whole embarrassing story. I was expecting Southern Baptist-style fire and brimstone, but Dad was as cool as a cucumber. Not a flicker of anger crossed his face. Instead, over Mom's country-fried steak, he broke it down with chilling precision.

"Getting in a hurry," he said, as Mom fried up one of my favorite meals, "is the fastest way to make mistakes." Then he gave me homework. Watch Isack Willis, his best tractor operator, and learn. "Watch how he moves," Dad said. "He seems slow, sure—but he gets more done in a day than anyone else. He's just so smooth."

Years later, Isack would end up working for me until he retired. He was—and still is—the best operator I've ever seen. And I really hope he gets to read this, because it's the solid gold truth.

At the time, I didn't realize Dad's advice was about more than just driving a tractor. It was a life lesson. So many of his teachings were like that. It took me years after he was gone to truly understand what he meant.

A few years ago, I came across a phrase used by the Navy SEALs: Slow is smooth, smooth is fast. I was reading Jocko Willink's book when it all clicked into place. That night at the table, eating Mom's cooking, wasn't just about avoiding mistakes in the field. It was about living with a steady, intentional pace—always moving. Movement is motivation. Everything good in life comes from moving.

Even now, I'll catch myself getting in a hurry and think back to that lesson. I see Isack in my mind, turning a big tractor around, his movements as smooth as glass. And I hear Dad's voice over dinner, steady and calm, reminding me: Slow is smooth. Smooth is fast.

CHAPTER 8

Bubbaisms

There's a photo of me and my dad somewhere in a scrapbook my sweet momma made for me. I'm about four or five years old. It's the two of us sitting in their bed in the same house I now own. Daddy wore glasses, so I was wearing some of his old ones to look like him. I had my legs crossed like his and my hands behind my head, just like him.

Many sons don't have a great relationship with their dads. I had thirty-two years with mine, and we never had an argument. He never once raised his voice in anger at me. We thought alike on many things—and on many, we didn't. We had our disagreements, sure, but we never argued. I got myself into trouble, but he never belittled me.

Daddy was a man's man in so many ways—tall, handsome, good at sports and hunting. Though by the time I was old enough to shoot my own gun, he had largely given up hunting because he loathed the cold. He was born on February 13 at home, not in a hospital. Mammy said the door blew open with a cold February wind just as he was born, and he had been cold ever since! Daddy's favorite book was *Dollar Cotton* by John Faulkner, William Faulkner's brother.

Daddy was a people person—when he was in the mood. Me too. He could hold his liquor and tell the best jokes you've ever heard. He had a presence in a crowd. He could rub elbows with kings or paupers and fit right in. He was a great golfer, sometimes playing eighteen holes in the morning and another eighteen in the afternoon. I once saw him shoot a hundred doves in a hundred shots with an old Browning over-and-under that I now own. He missed once but killed two in one shot to win a side bet he had going.

On his first date with my momma, he threw a quarter in the air and shot it with a .22 rifle. They found it, and my mom still has it sixty years later. It has a little dent right on the edge. I asked her what on earth she must've thought, and she said, "Now that's a man right there." He was confident—maybe even cocky—but somehow in an endearing way.

Daddy saw himself as an old-school gentleman planter rather than a yeoman farmer. He wore pressed khakis most days, along with neatly pressed button-up shirts. His shirts always had pockets. In one pocket, he kept a Cross pen, Salem cigarettes, and a little black leather-bound Farm Bureau journal. He wrote in that journal every day, and he kept them all. I have them now. His whole adult life sits on a shelf in my office.

March 5, 1977 – "Memphis to Vegas"

May 15, 1979 – "Planted Cotton"

May 24, 1979 – "Cold"

Sept 5, 1979 – "December Cotton sixty-five cents"

Sept 16, 1981 – "Church Finance Committee 9:30"

Daddy had a knack for staying clean. He'd walk into the shop in those pressed khakis, help out for a few minutes, and then head back to the office. I almost never saw him dirty. Don't get me wrong, he was dirty, but compared to the rest of us, he was sharp and clean. I'd be working on a motor with Thomas Hall, covered in grease from head to toe, and Daddy would still look spotless. It was like a magic trick.

Daddy also had the best one-liners—most of them advice disguised as jokes. I've started calling them Bubbaisms, and they are gold. Here are a few:

- "If your outgo exceeds your income, your upkeep will be your downfall."
- "Work with your brain, not with your back."
- "They have never charged what whiskey and cigarettes are worth, but they're getting mighty damn close!"
- "You can't take chicken shit and make chicken salad out of it."
- "Plant your corn early, and don't smoke in bed."
- "I work for myself, so nobody but my Daddy and my banker tells me what to do."
- "We're going to do something—even if it's wrong."

Dad adopted an African proverb as the motto for his farm. He had my Aunt Diane carefully write it out on parchment paper in elegant calligraphy. When you stepped into the office, there it was, proudly displayed for all to see:

> *"Every day in Africa, a lion wakes up. It knows it must run faster than the slowest gazelle or it will surely starve. Every day in Africa, a gazelle wakes up. It knows it must run faster than the fastest lion or it*

will surely be eaten. So, it doesn't matter whether you are a lion or a gazelle—when the sun rises, you better have your ass up and running."

Once, after hearing other farmers complain about tractor drivers not showing up for work, I commented on how lucky we were to have such a great team on our farm. Daddy replied, "Son, luck has nothing to do with it." That simple line stuck with me. His advice often came in one-liners like that—lessons you had to think about to fully understand. This one has guided me as an employer ever since: we treat our people right.

As a kid, I remember Mom cooking dinner every night. There was a rhythm to it. Dad would come in—with me in tow if it wasn't a school day—and she'd meet him at the door with a kiss, then start supper as she told him about her day. She even placed a recliner in the doorway between the kitchen and the breakfast nook so he could rest while she talked. We had a meat and three every night and rarely ate supper out. Aside from an occasional Saturday night meal at the Drew Country Club or ribs at the Ranchero in Clarksdale after a track meet, I don't ever remember my parents taking my sister and me out to eat when we were young.

It was always me, my sister Laura Dow, my mom, and my dad at that lime green table with metal chairs in the breakfast nook. I wouldn't trade those memories for the world.

One of the staples of our family dinners was Momma's pot roast—cooked low and slow with potatoes and carrots until the whole house smelled like comfort. There was always some left over, and the next night, without fail, we'd have open-faced roast beef sandwiches—one of Daddy's favorites. When I opened the restaurant, I put those sandwiches on the menu and named them after him: The Judge Bubba. At the time, he was serving as a justice court judge, and it felt like the perfect nod to the man behind the magic.

Delta Magazine picked up on the story and decided to feature the sandwich. They came out to do a full photo shoot, and by then, Daddy was undergoing chemo. It was one of his bad days—the kind where even standing took effort. But he showed up, wearing his strength like armor. He sat for the photos and pretended to enjoy the sandwich. He didn't want to be there; he wasn't even hungry. But I think he did it for me. That was the kind of man he was.

I've never been able to look at those photos or read the article. I don't want to remember him like that—tired and worn down from the chemo. I want to hold on to the image of him full of life, out on the farm, a cigarette in one hand, pressed khakis on, giving orders like a field general. That's the man I see when I think of him.

Daddy retired from farming in 1999. I don't think he really wanted to. He ran for justice court judge out of boredom. He was diagnosed with cancer in 2004 and passed away in 2006. The last life-changing quote I remember him saying was, "I am not afraid to die." He had just passed his sixty-third birthday. I was heartbroken.

My dad was my best friend, my hero, and my most important mentor.

CHAPTER 9

Father Figures

Having started life without a father, I was incredibly blessed to be adopted by Ann Dow and Bubba Shurden. For all the lessons my dad gave me, one of his greatest gifts was the many father figures he brought into my life through the farm. I was surrounded by strong, capable men—some family, some workers on the farm—but all of them left their mark on me. I don't think my exposure to them was accidental. Dad understood the value of these relationships, and that's one of the greatest gifts he left me.

I hesitate to name names because I know I'll leave someone out, but here are just a few of the men who helped raise me, and the lessons they taught me.

Thomas Hall. Mr. Thomas was a cornerstone of Dad's farm and a huge part of why it was so successful. Like Dad, he was meticulous—what we called "ticky"—and he was the best mechanic I've ever known. He taught me the importance of taking pride in my work. When I got older, he even showed me how to overhaul a diesel motor. Uncle Reggie had bought four of them at a farm sale, and we went to work in the shop. Those engines were in rough shape—oil likely never changed. We broke them down piece by piece. Every day, I went home with blackened clothes and oil on my face and hands—stains Ajax couldn't remove. The one time I wore gloves, he made fun of me, saying, "You must want soft hands so you don't tear the pantyhose on those girls you've been chasing."

Mr. Thomas preferred working alone when faced with a problem. It was how he thought things through—turning the puzzle over in his mind. Sometimes he'd even come to the shop on his day off to tinker and figure things out. One Christmas Eve, on an especially cold day, he went to the shop in his insulated coveralls. While sliding under a cotton picker head to check something, one of the spindles snagged his coveralls and trapped him. He never admitted how long he was stuck, but it was long enough for the farm's other manager, John Henry, to find him when he came by for a pipe wrench.

Today, when my nephew asks how to fix something, I'll often head to the shop early in the morning just to think, just like Mr. Thomas used to do. He taught me more than mechanics. Sure, I learned how to fix a dead bar on a cotton picker, overhaul a motor, and work with my hands. But mostly, he taught me how to solve problems on my own. That's a skill not taught much anymore. He showed me that good work is just as much about the effort you put in as it is about the result you get out.

John Henry Johnson. His name sounds like it belongs to a towering folk hero. But John Henry wasn't what you might expect. He was a gentle soul—steady, calm, and full of a patience that seemed limitless. The kind of patience you read about but rarely see in real life. He had an even keel that nothing could upset.

One of his hands told the story of his life—a thumb and no fingers, lost in a farm accident. But he never let it slow him down. On the farm, work was divided: Thomas handled the cotton while John Henry took care of the grain. That meant John Henry worked more directly for my Uncle Reggie. I tried calling him "Mr." once, and he wouldn't have it.

One summer, my dad decided I needed to learn a few lessons, so he told me I couldn't act like the boss's son. He wanted me to understand that I wasn't better than anyone working on the farm. That summer, I rode to work every day with John Henry. He picked me up first and dropped me off last—me, sandwiched between two grown tractor drivers in the back seat. It was humbling in the best way.

Back then, our bookkeeper, Mr. Billy, paid everyone in cash every Friday, handing out little manila envelopes. After a particularly long week, John Henry was driving me home when he asked, "What are you going to do with all that money?" It had been a good payday for me, at my new wage of two dollars an hour. The question seemed innocent, but I understood what he was really saying. The other guys on the farm had real bills—rent, groceries, utilities. Meanwhile, I had zero responsibilities. That two dollars an hour was all mine, just play money. In his gentle, understated way, John Henry was reminding me how good I had it. And he was right. I did.

When John Henry passed away, I stood at his funeral and told that story. It was just a small moment in a lifetime of them, but it stayed with me. It captured the kind of man he was—kind, patient, and quietly wise. A man who taught me lessons without ever needing to say much at all.

Charles Jackson. Every family has a fun uncle—we all know exactly what I mean. Mine was Uncle Charles, also a farmer. He was married to my dad's oldest sister, Aunt Nell. He wore a short-brimmed cowboy hat, chewed plug tobacco, and was a craftsman with talent bordering on artistry. His son, Bill, is, in fact, a professional artist.

Uncle Charles loved watching old footage of himself playing football in high school. He rode a motorcycle back then, and from what I've heard, Granddaddy Reg didn't know what to think when he showed up at the house to pick up Aunt Nell.

One winter, Dad decided we needed to build about thirty small bridges so our irrigation center pivots could cross the ditches without getting stuck. We had tried wood before, with little success, so Dad decided to go with metal I-beams. The thing was—I didn't know how to weld.

Uncle Charles spent a couple of days in the shop teaching me. He was a skilled welder, always building something in his own shop. When I was spraying Johnson grass on my four-wheeler, he even built me a little trailer for the spray rig, so I could unhook it and go fishing when it rained.

Learning to weld on the new steel was pretty straightforward. We both had on helmets. He explained which rod worked best with which type of steel. I'd stand as close as I could, watching him, then try to mimic what he did while he watched me. During one of our lessons, I was watching him with my helmet on when I smelled smoke. I lifted the helmet, and my grease-stained coveralls were on fire! I was fine, and we all got a good laugh out of it.

A couple of years ago, we broke a large drum that went on a combine header. No one wanted to weld it—it was likely to fail. Ordering a new one would take two weeks. So I did what Uncle Charles would have done:

I welded it myself. And it worked. Mr. Mike Ellis saw it and said, "Thomas Hall and Charles Jackson sure would be proud of you."

Reggie Shurden. Reggie Shurden is my dad's brother and was his partner on the farm. He moved back to Drew after Granddaddy Reg passed away and started farming with Daddy. I don't think he ever realized how cool I thought he was back then. He had a weight set in the driveway at Mammy's house, and he used to burp loudly just to make me laugh.

He married Judy in a small wedding, and they had two sons, Reg and Heath. Aunt Judy was a beautiful woman, and Heath looks so much like her. Sadly, Aunt Judy got cancer and passed away in 1991, leaving Reggie to raise their two young sons.

Years later, I replaced John Henry on the farm as Reggie's manager. In many ways, Reggie was the opposite of Daddy. He definitely had a temper. I say "had" because now he has two granddaughters who have softened him up. Back then, though, he was tough to work for (more on those days later). Still, much of the way I approach farming doesn't come from Daddy, but from the years I spent working directly under Uncle Reggie. The man taught me a lot about farming and is the best rice farmer I've ever known. These days, we're close, and I often go to him for advice and counsel. I'm grateful for the years I spent working with him.

Fred Strehle. Uncle Fred was married to my dad's sister, Diane. They lived across the road from my Uncle Charles and Aunt Nell, right on Highway 49—about six hundred feet from where I used to cross the highway to mow Mammy's yard. Fred also ran the family cotton gin until new regulations forced it to close in 1991.

By the time I was old enough to really hunt with a gun, Daddy had mostly given it up. Uncle Fred stepped in and took me hunting with his two sons, Dallas and Adam, and their dog, Sue.

Sue, a Lab with unusually short legs, was often underestimated, though she was usually the star of any dove or duck hunt. Uncle Fred liked to joke that Sue could smell game better because her short legs kept her nose closer to the ground.

Every time Uncle Fred took Dallas and Adam dove hunting, he never failed to include me. I spent so much time at their house that Dallas and Adam aren't just my cousins—they're some of my closest friends.

Opening day of dove season was an event that mattered in the Delta. Farmers spread wheat across their fields to lure the migratory mourning doves. Some, like us, went a step further and planted entire crops of sunflowers. By mid-July, you could drive the backroads of the Mississippi Delta and spot patches of bright yellow stretching across the horizon. Those fields became backdrops for countless family photos, capturing the beauty of the Delta in full bloom. By the first weekend of September, the sunflowers had dried, and the doves arrived by the thousands, their migration turning fields into gathering places for fathers, sons, and whole families alike.

This wasn't just about hunting. It was a social occasion that brought people home—a reunion of friends and family from across the country. Truck radios blared SEC football games, the unofficial soundtrack of early fall, and some farmers even hosted live bands in their fields after the day's hunt.

For the Shurden family, opening day followed a familiar rhythm. Relatives came from all corners, drawn back to Shurden Farms for the tradition. When the sun dipped low over the flat Delta fields, we'd head back to Mammy's house to clean the day's harvest. There, in her small kitchen, she fried the doves in her favorite black iron skillet. She served them with cathead biscuits, rice and gravy, fresh-sliced tomatoes, and fried okra picked from her garden that morning.

Granddaddy Reg always said grace, his voice steady and certain, and we gathered around the table to eat. There were no bands playing, no grand celebrations then. It was simpler: faith, farming, family, and food—the kind of moments that stay with you long after the last plate is cleared. Those meals were more than food; they were the best parts of life served at a kitchen table.

CHAPTER 10

Go West, Young Man

My dad always had a thing for cowboy movies, and I spent a lot of evenings in the house with him watching John Wayne and Clint Eastwood, longing for the adventures they had. Dad often lamented that he was born a hundred years too late. When Indiana Jones came along, I found my own version of adventure, often wishing I'd been born years earlier to traverse the world wearing a fedora rather than a cowboy hat. Dad and I shared a sense of adventure that I honestly never recognized until I started writing this book.

In the '80s in Mississippi, you could get your full driver's license just thirty days after turning fifteen. By then, I'd already been driving for a while, so going to the Mississippi Highway Patrol office in Cleveland to take the test didn't feel like a big deal. I passed on my fifteenth birthday and got my license that July.

Dad handed me the keys to his little S-10 Chevrolet Blazer, and just like that, I was off. Moving from a four-wheeler to a real vehicle felt like a promotion to a new world of independence. My parents trusted me. Some of that trust came from the times we lived in, but a lot of it was earned. I never broke curfew or came home smelling like alcohol.

Friday nights in Drew meant cruising the "Big Block." That was the loop—Park Avenue to Third Street to South Boulevard to Main Street and back again. We'd stop at the Sunflower Food Store parking lot until Pinky, one of Drew's finest, rolled up to run us off. Then we'd circle back to Drew High School, where Pinky—or maybe Barney Fife or Chief—would be waiting to chase us off again. It was all in good fun. We had nicknames for the cops, but they were decent guys who knew how to let kids be kids.

I went to a private school, but Drew High's parking lot was our melting pot—public and private school kids hanging out, talking, becoming friends. Years later, when I ran for judge, people would come up to me and say, "We went to Drew High together." I'd just nod and laugh. Gen X was cool like that.

Most nights, we'd end up on Highway 49 at the Rebel Roost. It was a cinder block drive-in painted that odd shade of institutional green you see on government buildings and high school walls. I figure it got its name because hometown hero, Archie Manning, was playing football at Ole Miss when it was built. The Rebel Roost was a classic Southern dairy bar with a front window where you could order burgers, malts, or milkshakes. When the weather was nice, we sat on car hoods waiting for our food—a scene that played out all across the South. On colder nights, we'd wander to the back door and step into a small dining room with a game room tucked away, but we preferred being outside, just far enough from adult supervision to feel free.

The Rebel Roost's chili cheeseburger with slaw was a legend—messy, salty, and best chased with a milkshake. I must've eaten a thousand of them. The place closed in 2005, but we run a chili cheeseburger special now and then at the restaurant as a small tribute to those days: The Roost Burger.

Having a car meant the world opened up. We drove to Cleveland to hang out and found a little shack called Crawdads in Merigold, selling crawfish off the front porch. Back then, it wasn't a steakhouse—just a spot to grab something spicy and good. We discovered country stores, places my four-wheeler couldn't reach, each with its own charm and quirks.

There was the Mecca—Ruleville's answer to the Rebel Roost—and River Road, one of my all-time favorites. River Road had chicken strips that were unmatched and something I'd never seen before: fried cheese. At fifteen, that seemed like the pinnacle of culinary creativity. We'd often skip lunch at school just to make it to River Road by three for those chicken strips and cheese sticks.

Having wheels made hunting a whole lot easier, too. There's something about having a warm ride to and from the duck hole that changes the game entirely. Ducks were my main focus back then. Deer hunting wasn't great in the '80s, but duck hunting was incredible. In truth, I would hunt any game you could shake salt and pepper on. If it was in season, I was hunting it.

In eleventh grade, Bill Melton moved to Drew to live with his dad, the chief of police. You couldn't find two people more different than me and Bill: music, drinking, politics—we didn't see eye to eye on much of anything. But there's something about watching a dozen mallards cupped over your decoys with a Delta sunrise lighting up the horizon. It bonds you in a way that's hard to explain. Back then, we had plenty of ducks on the farm, and we harvested our fair share.

That's probably when I first started cooking. If you've ever had wild game, you know it's a flavor all its own. People call it gamey, but ducks take that to another level. As a good steward of what we hunted, I wanted to figure out how to make them taste good.

I started simple. I'd wrap the duck breasts in bacon, stuff them with cream cheese and jalapeño, and cook them on Dad's grill. Sometimes I'd take them to the Piggly Wiggly, where my friend Phil would run the filets through the minute steak tenderizer. We'd fry them up and smother them in gravy.

My favorite was learning to make duck gumbo. I picked up Mom's copy of the *Pick of the Crop* cookbook and taught myself how to make a roux. If you can find a copy of that cookbook, you've struck gold, my friend. Mrs. Grittman's gumbo recipe is the real deal. These days I have a lot more recipes in my repertoire, but that bacon-wrapped duck and the duck gumbo are still my go-to.

Those early experiments in the kitchen weren't just about making ducks edible—they were the start of something bigger, a love for cooking that's stuck with me ever since. Mom was mostly cool about letting me experiment in her kitchen, although she often got a little upset with my cleaning skills. (Sorry, Mom!)

I also graduated to become a full-fledged worker on the farm. I had learned a lot and was as good a tractor driver as most. I could plow a straight line, and I was dependable. I could do the math on chemicals. I was also now paid full minimum wage: $3.35 an hour.

I remember the summer I turned sixteen, Daddy came and got me off the tractor and took me to K-Mart in Cleveland. He told me to pick out any rod and reel I wanted. That was the only time he ever did anything like that, and I loved that rod and reel. We checked out, and he took me back to the tractor so I could finish the day's work.

For the rest of my high school years, I continued much like this. I'd work on the farm driving a tractor and plowing cotton during the summer and on weekends, saving up my money to go adventuring. My friends and I would hunt and travel, and hunt and travel. I am so grateful for my childhood and the amount of room my parents gave me to fail and grow. I would not trade those years for anything.

But let me be real clear: I was also the pimple-faced runt of the litter.

I loved my high school days, but I also had to work really hard to be liked and to fit in. I loved girls, too, but in those days, getting them to return the favor was not easy. I became a salesman very early in life, chasing connection and acceptance in every conversation. I suppose I just learned to present the best version of myself to people, to connect on the level they wanted to connect. I learned that connection was not about me but about the person I was trying to connect with. By graduation, I loved my classmates, and they loved me, and while I wouldn't trade that experience, I also wouldn't want to go back and live it again.

The only place I really felt like myself was out on that farm—working, hunting, or cooking with friends and family. *Faith, family, farming, food*— the ties that bind.

CHAPTER 11

College Knowledge

I always knew two things: I'd go to Mississippi State University, and I'd farm like my daddy. Daddy never pressured me to farm, but when it came to college, he laid it on pretty thick. I'll never forget him saying, "You can go to any college you want, but if you want me to help pay for it, you're going to Starkville." He was kidding, of course—but he didn't have to be. I wanted to go.

After a pretty memorable SAE GJ Faulkner fraternity rush party during our senior year of high school, so did my friend, Dean.

Dean moved to Drew in 1979, and our moms became best friends. We'd been inseparable since first grade and stayed that way all through college at Mississippi State. Our friendship was steady, built on shared memories and a bond that never really wavered. Dean was cool. His stepdad, Tommy Miller, built bike ramps behind their house, and we all skinned a knee there. I still have a picture in my mind of Dean on his BMX bike wearing his Evel Knievel costume. Dean and everyone else called Mr. Tommy "Pops."

That SAE party sealed the deal for Dean. He applied to Mississippi State, and before long, we were touring the campus together. It was beautiful. McCool Hall, where the Business School was housed, was nicknamed the "McCool Country Club"—and it wasn't hard to see why. But the freshman dorms? That was another story.

Calling those dorms "bad" would be like calling a prison cell "austere." If those old dorms had been at Parchman, the ACLU would've been all over it. Mississippi State's freshman dorms today are like high-end apartments, but back then? They were works of cruel art. Dean and I couldn't stomach the thought of living there.

So, we schemed. We crunched numbers like sharks at a poker table and found a set of budget-friendly apartments on the edge of town called Canterbury. We pitched the idea to our parents: the dorms were intolerable, we'd save money cooking in our own kitchen, and it just made sense. No PowerPoint back then, but we put together the closest thing.

Crazy thing is—it worked. By the fall of 1991, Dean and I were the only freshmen at Mississippi State with our own apartment. Canterbury became our home—and everyone else's hangout. It was a magnet for our friends, and we made it work on a shoestring budget. Our bathroom even had a toll system: admission was a roll of toilet paper. The freshman dorm bathrooms were that bad.

Living at Canterbury was the time of my life. The friendships forged there have lasted decades: Danny, Lee, Blake, Mitch, Andy, Whit, Riley—the list goes on. We cooked, we laughed, and we learned a lot about life.

Lee once made a stew with whatever protein he could scrounge up by knocking on every door in the complex—beef, chicken, wild game—and stirred it with a broom handle in the courtyard. Someone baked cornbread to go with it. Lee dragged his recliner into the center courtyard and spent the day stirring the pot. That night, everyone who contributed to the stew came out and ate together. We also had a Friendsgiving the day before everyone went home for Thanksgiving. No alcohol allowed. I blessed the food.

I cooked a lot, too. Mom gifted me my very own *Pick of the Crop* cookbook, so I was indeed using our kitchen. I made a really good chili and country-fried steak—though I never quite mastered the gravy.

Danny introduced me to Asian food. Starkville had a full-menu Chinese restaurant, and while I'd had egg rolls before, most of my meals had been country cooking. It didn't take long for me to develop a taste for egg drop soup and General Tso's chicken. Not long after, a Chinese buffet opened up, and for broke college kids, it was heaven. Still, we couldn't stay away from a good meat and three. The Starkville Café became a regular stop for us, offering a taste of home when we needed it most.

By my last year in Starkville, I had a routine figured out. Business School meant a lot of adults were enrolled, and that meant night classes. I took a Monday night class, a Wednesday night class, and two Tuesday/Thursday classes. I also went to Classics in Columbus for country night on Wednesdays after class, and to Cheers on Thursday night for their own country night. Since I didn't drink, I drove everyone. That meant no school on Fridays, and no school on Mondays until my evening class.

During harvest, I'd head home after class on Thursday and work on the farm. During duck season, I'd do the same—getting in all the duck hunting I could.

While in college, I spent a lot of time reading things like *The Art of the Deal* and *Think and Grow Rich*. I also delved into some fly-by-night stuff too—books on buying real estate with no money down. I can't remember the author's name, but I saw him on the news one night being arrested for scamming people out of their money. Lesson learned. My friend, Sandra, joked that I'd probably be the Donald Trump of Drew. We laughed, not knowing then that he'd end up in politics.

Looking back, I wasn't exactly focused on school. My schedule was designed for fun, farming, hunting, and food. By the spring of my fourth year, my dad sat me down for a talk I'll never forget. There was a tear in his eye when he told me that college wasn't for everyone. I was not making the grades I should, nor was I on schedule to graduate on time, and maybe I should come home, work full-time on the farm, and finish my degree at Delta State.

That conversation still messes with me. I was a young man who thought he had it all figured out, and in that moment, I realized I'd let the old man down. I carry that with me even now, at an age not much different from his back then. It's left me with a chip on my shoulder. A big one. It's made me tough and gritty, but it's always there, just beneath the surface. Don't let the charm fool you.

CHAPTER 12

Back to the Delta

On April Fools' Day 1995, I met Leslie Davis from Indianola at the Catfish Festival in Belzoni. That night, under a clear sky, we saw a shooting star. I knew then I would marry her. There was never a question after that night. I also knew I'd be returning home to work on the farm and finish my degree at Delta State. It felt like fate. Everything seemed to be coming together.

If I was moving home, I needed a place to live. My friends, Bill and Chris, were also looking, and there was this big, old house out on a farm my dad rented. It looked a lot like the one from the Amityville Horror movie. It had been vacant for years and belonged to the estate of my great-uncle Otha. I called my cousin, Shurden, and we struck a deal: if I would repair the property and take care of the massive yard, I could live there rent-free. That sounded good enough to me.

Calling the house "rough" would be putting it lightly. Chris and I lived in the main part of the house, and Bill stayed in the attic. That's right—the attic. The only air conditioning came from a few window units: one in each bedroom and one in the den where we watched TV. The kitchen? It didn't even have cabinets. Shurden's sister, Tracy, had them removed with plans to replace them, but she ended up moving into another house owned by the estate and left the kitchen as it was.

The AC in my room was a literal fire hazard, running off a 75-foot extension cord plugged into the kitchen. The kitchen itself had only a stand-alone sink and a stove sitting by itself on one wall. But we were a group of young guys—we made it work.

The house was supposedly haunted. People said a little girl had died there and still haunted the property. It had been built in the early twentieth century by the Smith family, though I couldn't find anyone who remembered exactly when. Uncle Otha bought the farm years later and let the Smith brothers stay as long as they wanted. Ot Smith, one of the brothers, lived in the house we were now calling home.

Ot was a character. Stories about him bordered on legend. They said he once dug up a skeleton from a nearby Indian mound, pieced it together, and took it to a museum in Jackson. When the museum offered to store it in the basement, Ot refused, loaded it back into his truck, and brought it home to re-bury. He also had a strange fondness for rat snakes, catching them on the farm and releasing them in the attic to control the mice. Another story claimed he invented a .22 machine gun, figuring cheap ammo would appeal to militaries. I have no idea if any of this is true, but the tales about Ot were endless.

When I moved in, the house wasn't just rough—it was ridiculous. Every room was some shade of pink. My Uncle Charles came by one day, looked around, and said, "You weren't kidding. That's titty pink right there!" I joked with Tracy that she must've been going through a serious pink phase. She and I had a good laugh.

Over time, we cleaned the place up. I painted over the pink, built cabinets for the kitchen, and installed proper window units. Les and I married on June 29, 1996—the day before I turned twenty-three. Chris and Bill had moved on by then, and Les transformed the old house into something beautiful. Interior decorating is her gift. It looked like a dream home when we entertained friends, but the reality was far different.

Summers were unbearably hot, and the house was infested with mosquitoes. Winters were brutal. One time, we stayed with my parents because the heater couldn't keep up, and my towel from the night before was frozen solid on the floor, with a little ice forming in the toilet.

The house had its quirks. Lights flickered. A room would have a cold spot in the middle of July. Late at night, we'd hear footsteps in the attic. One night, Les woke up screaming that someone was in the room with us. I jumped out of bed and ripped the light off the wall in my haste to turn it on. There was no one there. I called it a bad dream, but Les wasn't so sure. Another time, I felt warm breath on the back of my neck while in the bathroom. That was enough for us to leave the house for the night.

Sometimes, when the lights flickered, I'd talk to Ot. I'd say, "Now, Ot, if you keep this up, I'm going to move out and let Tracy paint this place pink again." I swear the lights would stop. I don't really believe in ghosts, but strange things happened, man.

The house was a perfect metaphor for my early years back in Drew. From the outside, it seemed like I had it all together. The house looked grand, and Les decorated it like something out of *Southern Living*. But inside, it was hot in the summer, freezing in the winter, and seemed haunted in more ways than one. I was barely scraping by financially, making it work, but struggling every step of the way.

Since money was tight, we didn't eat out much. Sitting in the den of the Smith house, we became obsessed with the Food Network—especially Emeril Lagasse. I sat in an old recliner Les's dad had given me. The back was broken, so to recline, I'd move it away from the wall, and then back again to sit up straight. I'd done this so many times the wall was rubbed bare where the recliner rested against it.

We watched *Emeril Live* every night and tried so many of his recipes in the early years of our marriage—étouffée, shrimp and grits, gumbo, and countless others using ingredients in new ways. It was a lot of fun! I have to give a nod to Emeril for shaping how I think about food today. It might sound clichéd, but his influence is alive in my restaurant on Main Street in Drew, right alongside Mammy's.

Emeril showed me that really great cooking doesn't have to be hard or pretentious. As he put it, "We aren't building rocket ships here."

PART II

Try, Fail, Learn

CHAPTER 13

Straw Boss

I remember the call over the radio. We were moving pivots out on the farm. Not many people do that anymore—it's backbreaking work—but back then, it was common. We all had CB radios in our trucks, and I still remember John Henry coming over the air: "Mr. Bubba, I don't feel too good. I'm gonna lay down here on this concrete."

It didn't sound right, and we all knew it. I don't remember who got to him first, but they drove him straight to Ruleville Hospital. John Henry had a heart attack—and a bad one. A helicopter flew him from Ruleville to Jackson and saved his life. He lived another fifteen years, but he could no longer work on the farm.

Aunt Judy had passed just a couple of years earlier, and now Reggie's right-hand man couldn't work. It was a tough spot for him. Over the next few years, Reggie went through a string of managers. The last one left around the time I transferred to Delta State.

One night, Dad called me to come talk. Reggie was thinking about quitting farming, and Daddy didn't want to do it alone. They were partners. They decided to let me be the manager and work directly for

Reggie. That meant I had to drop out of school. I was pretty close to graduating. All I needed was Banking and Finance and Ethics.

I joke now that I've borrowed and repaid millions of dollars, and I was a judge for fourteen years, so I think I've got those covered. Still, I have some regret about quitting so close to the finish line. Dad later admitted that pressuring me to leave was a mistake, but I understood. The circumstances were tough.

So, I became the manager, taking John Henry's place for $1,000 a month. Six months later, Les and I got married.

Dad told me a couple of things right off the bat. First, even though I had grown up on the farm and worked hard beside everyone, I shouldn't expect or ask for their respect—I had to earn it by outworking them. Second, "outworking" meant the day no longer started at 7 a.m., but at 6:30.

Me, Mr. Thomas, Daddy, and Uncle Reggie would meet at the shop every morning at 6:30 to go over the day's goals. To this day, I still come to work at 6:30. Being on time is a big deal to me. I just don't understand tardiness. I was a judge for fourteen years and never started court late. Being on time shows discipline and respect. It's a contract between you and the person you made a promise to.

My coach, Michael Burt, always says, "Discipline comes from the word *disciple*… to give yourself fully to a person or cause you believe in." There is no better way to show someone you are committed than being on time. Being late is another way of saying, "This is not that important to me. You are not that important to me."

The next time I saw my grandmother, Mammy, she said, "I heard they made you straw boss." I had never heard that term before. Writing this today, I googled it. A straw boss was in charge of the wheat straw—the less valuable part of the wheat. The term has come to mean someone in charge, but not really in charge. I don't think Mammy meant it that way, but that's exactly what it was.

To be blunt, Reggie didn't really trust me to handle things. Maybe that was fair. I was fiercely independent, and Uncle Reggie was a micromanager. It wasn't a great mix.

Still, I enjoyed being "straw boss." I loved the size of our farm. It was big. We had a lot of machinery and a lot of employees. There was always something to do—I was never idle. People who don't know about farming imagine slow but hard work. In truth, there's an urgency to farming that I love. There's always a deadline. I work well with deadlines. I thrive under pressure.

Our planting window for the crops is narrow. Beans planted at a certain time out-yield those planted later. Same with corn and rice. There's always a weather system we're trying to beat. In the fall, it's the same. Our crops mature just as hurricane season starts. We're like sailors, navigating huge machines through an ocean of grain, eyes on the forecast. I like the pressure.

One time we were chasing planters, and Reggie came by and reset the planters I had just set. I didn't think much of it at the time. But the next day, he came out and told me he hadn't slept much because he was worried I might have had them set right to begin with. It was his way of apologizing, and I appreciated it. He was starting to trust me. That was four years in. That's how long it took.

I'm not complaining—I want to be clear about that. Reggie was the best rice farmer I've ever met. This was before we had the hybrid varieties available today, and we were getting yields no one would believe. I'm a much better farmer because of his influence, and I owe him a ton.

The days of working for Reggie were long, but I still looked forward to lunch and a brief reprieve from the hot summer sun with friends and mentors, Uncle Reggie included. Sullivan's had closed when I was in college, so we ate most of our lunches at the Rebel Roost. But my friend, Timbo, was opening a brand-new gas station on Highway 49, just across from our shop. It had a full restaurant inside, and his mom, Miss Jo Ann, ran the kitchen. On Thursdays, she cooked fried ribs. I had never even heard of fried ribs at the time—and they were amazing. All the food was.

Years later, Miss Jo Ann would work for me at Stafford's Market and teach us how to make those fried ribs. We sold so many that I even printed T-shirts that said: *"Jo Ann's World Famous Fried Ribs!"*

I ate at Timbo's every day. The food was so good. The place was new and clean, with a huge gravel side lot for big trucks. At some point, Timbo and I struck a deal—I'd keep the lot graded and clean, and I'd get to eat for free. At $1,000 a month, that deal meant a lot. I ate a lot of gas station food for the next four years.

I love my restaurant, but I still miss that place. Sitting there with all the farmers, breaking bread, learning from them. Eating Miss Jo Ann's cooking. Those were good times. Faith, farming, family, and food.

CHAPTER 14

My Turn

I don't know what I expected to happen working for my uncle and dad. A part of me thought there would eventually be an opportunity to have some stake or ownership, or maybe a raise in pay that made me feel like I had ownership. That was never offered or discussed.

I was hungry in every way a young man could be. But I never told my dad that. I never asked. That's a huge lesson. I understand now that he would have been proud of me if I had asked. But I didn't. It's foolish to assume someone else understands how you feel or what your goals are.

Right now, there's someone in your life you know—deep down—you need to have a conversation with. Do it. Learn from my mistakes. Speak up. Bosses rarely know what you need, but we do care.

By 1999, my fourth year working with them as a manager, I had become pretty convinced I'd have to leave and start my own farm. I wanted to be "the guy." I wanted to be a farmer, not a manager. I had heard about some land becoming available and had been thinking it over. I had also heard about first-time farmer loans you could get from the government, like SBA loans, but for farmers. I played with the numbers, but I just couldn't make them work.

Another thing was—Les was pregnant. I had to provide at a higher level. The old, cold Smith house was no place to raise a baby, and we made so little that we signed up for government assistance just to afford baby formula. I wasn't a great communicator back then, but I don't think Daddy or Reggie knew how much we were struggling. I'm one of those people who never complain—I'm always happy and smiling. That can be a blessing and a curse.

Just as the crop was starting to mature in 1999, my dad asked me to come by the house one evening. It felt a lot like the night he asked me to quit school. I could just tell—something big was about to happen.

Les was about six months pregnant, I was looking for land to start my own farm, and we were renovating and adding heat to the spare bedroom whenever I wasn't working. It was a weird time.

I walked into my dad's house. He was in his usual spot, and Momma was cooking. I sat down, and he told me that he and Reggie were retiring. In all fairness, life had been hard on Reggie—way too hard. He had two boys, Reg and Heath, who deserved more of his time. And he was at the point where he could sell out and give them that. It was the right thing to do.

Daddy didn't really want to quit. We discussed the possibility of me buying out Reggie. Reggie was willing to give me a great deal—he truly appreciated me. It was a sweetheart deal. There I was, twenty-six years old, making $1,000 a month, and the amount just felt huge at the time. It was the best deal I've ever been offered by anyone—and I was afraid. I turned it down. I took door number two.

Door number two was Daddy and Reggie retiring, and me renting their land and starting a brand-new farm. They gave me two huge legs up. First,

I had the first pick of all the land they farmed, so I chose the grain farm just north of Drew. Then they sold me two tractors, a planter, a disk, and a couple of irrigation motors—and financed them for me. Everything else went into the sale in Webb. In a matter of just a couple of months, Shurden Brothers Inc. was no more, and Stafford Shurden Farms was just beginning.

I have few real regrets, but not taking the deal Reggie offered is the biggest. Farming was really good over the next few years, and financially, it would have been a great decision. I also would have stepped right into a strong business with a solid system of people and procedures. That farm ran as smoothly and efficiently as a sewing machine.

Then there was the added benefit of being able to farm alongside my hero—my dad. I had no idea then that we only had a few years left with him. Every time I've played it small in life, I've later regretted it.

That said, I had a good start farming on my own, and those early years of Stafford Shurden Farms are still some of the best years of my life. The next couple of years were nothing but fun!

CHAPTER 15

First Year Luck

I did, in fact, get a first-time farmer loan from the USDA. One of the requirements was that you couldn't qualify for a traditional loan due to a lack of equity. I was living in a rented house, and even my wife's car was a lease. The only thing I owned was a fourteen-foot jon boat with an old, worn-out motor.

The loan officer looked at my budget and said, "I don't see any income for you. You have to set yourself a salary."

I hadn't really thought about it and just blurted out, "What about $2,000 a month?"

When I got home, I told my wife we were rich. It was meant as a joke, and we laughed, but it was also a doubling of income for our new family, and we were glad to get it.

Another benefit was getting to pick a farm worker. Dad had three top-tier guys, but I wasn't going to be able to afford them. I just needed a really good tractor driver. I asked Larry Hannon to come work with me.

The guys on the farm called Larry "Blackbird." Larry grew up on the farm and, in fact, was born out there near the old pole barn shop we had when

I was a kid. All that old land is covered in trees now. The pole barn and old houses have been erased from memory. Larry lives in town these days. He worked for me until he was sixty-seven and could draw his retirement. He's one of the nicest, most easygoing people I know.

That first year was a huge change. Going from a large farm with lots of tractors and workers to a small operation with just one guy was different. I had lots of free time. I wasn't working hundred-hour weeks anymore. We had one or two hard weeks in the spring. I didn't have a combine, so I paid my neighbor, Ricky Williamson, to harvest my crop.

I had time to play golf with my dad a couple times a week, and the pressure was much less. I joined the Chamber of Commerce and ended up on the board. I stayed up at night feeding our new baby. I had a huge garden—something I loved but never had time for before. I fished and hunted more. In all honesty, I was bored.

Dad also spent a lot of time on the farm with me. It was clear he missed it, but he was also obviously proud of the work I was doing. The crop was pretty and clean, and he was my mentor and advisor on a daily basis. He kept me moving in the right direction.

At the end of the year, I sat down with my accountant. She told me I'd had a good year—I made $100,000. We had been paying some taxes in, but I still owed $17,000 to the IRS. I had $27,000 in the bank, and all my crops were sold. That meant that after paying the IRS, I'd only have $10,000 left. I didn't really understand it at the time. It was a great lesson: profit and cash are two totally different things. Years later, a wise man told me, "You can't spend profit—you can only spend cash."

Still, I had not only survived my first year of farming—I had paid myself double, had more time for my family, and came out with a little extra money. I also kept my deal going with Timbo for free lunch, so I was starting to put on a few pounds for the first time in my life. Life was good.

CHAPTER 16

The Bored Farmer

The next couple of years on the farm passed much like the first. Days came and went in a steady rhythm, fields stretching endlessly under a Delta sky that could make you feel small or invincible, depending on the day. The work was honest, but the hours in between left me restless. I started spending more of my free time getting involved in the life of Drew.

The town was facing the same struggles as every rural place in the Delta. Opportunities had dried up, and the best of us left for Nashville, Oxford, or somewhere farther still. That exodus left a vacuum: of leadership, of investment, of energy. A hollowness that grew with every passing year. But if you stayed and wanted to help, people noticed. They needed young blood, and I wanted to matter.

I wasn't just adopted by Bubba and Ann Dow. This little town had taken me in, too. And I didn't want to see it die while I sat idly by. That felt wrong.

In 2001, Drew joined the Mississippi Main Street Program, a statewide effort to breathe life back into downtowns. "The downtown is the heart and soul of a town," they told us. But I didn't need convincing—I already believed it. A group of us, led by Mayor Jim Pettigrew, bought into the dream of bringing Drew back to life. It felt like a fight worth fighting.

That belief carried me into the idea of buying the old Sklar building from Jack Windam. It was one of those places that stuck with you, even after it had seen better days. When I was a kid, Phillip Sklar ran what he called an "antique store" there, although he sold more than just antiques. I have an old advertisement of his that says, "*We buy anything.*" Everybody called him "Pincus." He had a way about him—a salesman's instinct that bordered on genius.

Late at night, Pincus would load up his delivery truck with furniture from his own shop and slip out of town. The next morning, he'd drive back in, parading through the streets with the truck piled high. Word would spread like wildfire that Pincus had new stuff. By noon, the women of Drew were picking his shelves clean.

After WWII, Pincus bought a stash of surplus gas masks. The boys in town all had one, running through the fields playing army, their breath fogging up the lenses. It was the kind of story people told and retold—the kind that made Drew feel like home. But by 2001, Sklar's was long gone, and the building was falling apart.

I had a little cash saved up from winters spent guiding duck hunts, so I offered Mr. Jack $8,800 for it—all the cash I had access to. He turned me down flat. I figured that was the end of it. But a few months later, Mr. Jack flagged me down in the middle of the road. He'd been thinking about what I was trying to do. He said he wanted to help. He'd sell me the building for $8,800 after all.

We closed the deal in early 2002. I was now the proud owner of the Sklar building at 119 North Main Street—a structure with no electricity, no plumbing, no heat or air, and a roof that leaked like a sieve. Dad took one look at it and said, "You can't take chicken shit and make chicken salad out of it."

Maybe he was right. But it didn't matter. I was invested now, not just in that building, but in Drew's future. I knew what I wanted to do. I was gonna open a restaurant.

CHAPTER 17

Shurden Construction Co

In 2002, I expanded the farming operation—renting the Bordofski place and adding a combine and grain cart to my equipment list. Mike Mitchell—everyone called him "Spot"—came to work for me, a familiar face who had once worked for Dad. Farming was good. Dad was still around, always the trusted advisor, the steady hand.

When the rains came, as they always do, farming paused. That's when we traded the fields of Shurden Farms for 119 North Main. Larry, Mike, and I became a three-man construction crew, rebuilding the old Sklar building piece by piece. We pulled wire and ran plumbing, repairing decades of neglect with our own hands. The windows were shattered, their frames rotting, so we tore them out and rebuilt every one from scratch. When it came time for the roof, we installed metal, cutting and fitting it ourselves. Guy Cox, who owned the HVAC shop down the street, let me use his equipment to make custom flashing. We joked we were now Shurden Construction Co. with exactly one client and no profit margin.

Inside, the beautiful beaded ceiling was a mess. Years of water damage and time had warped and ruined much of it, and finding a match seemed impossible. Down the street, the Chamber of Commerce was renovating the old Fred's building. They had the same kind of ceiling, but instead of restoring it, they decided to cover it with a drop ceiling. They dumped the old boards that had come loose in a bin behind the building. I didn't think twice—I climbed into that dumpster and hauled out every salvageable piece. When we finished the ceiling at 119 North Main, we had exactly one board left. Just one. It felt like a sign that this was meant to be.

119 North Main didn't have HVAC—not even ductwork. Guy Cox helped again, this time with a tip: John Henry's cousin, Pie Johnson, had an HVAC unit for sale. Pie was the son of Doc Johnson, a man whose reputation spanned the full spectrum, depending on who you asked. Witch doctor, voodoo man, hoodoo man—it didn't matter what you called him. People came to Doc from all over the world to be healed. He made good money at it, too, leaving behind a comfortable inheritance for his kids.

Pie was a character in his own right. He'd buy anything he thought he could flip for a profit. This time, it was a wrecked eighteen-wheeler loaded with brand-new HVAC systems. The insurance company sold him the lot, and Guy and I made the drive to see him. We struck a deal: $1,500 cash. Guy had some leftover ductwork from another job, and just like that, 119 North Main had air conditioning. Doc and Pie are long gone now. The old house is gone too. But farmers name fields, and that one is still called The Voodoo Cut.

You read that right—the HVAC in 119 North Main came from a voodoo man living outside the town of Drew.

Rainy days and slow seasons stretched into two years of work. Slowly but surely, the building transformed. What had once been a neglected relic of Drew's past was now something to be proud of. 119 North Main was alive again.

CHAPTER 18

Main Street Deli & Gifts

There were already two restaurants in Drew in 2004. The Rebel Roost was still open, serving its daily meat and three alongside those famous chili cheeseburgers. Walter's had opened that same year. A friend of mine saw the same need I did—for downtown Drew to have a place to eat and, maybe more importantly, a place to fellowship. Walter's was a cafeteria-style buffet, the kind of spot where you went through the line and Walter or his wife, Miss Jesse, fixed your plate. You paid at the end based on what you got. Neckbones and collard greens were on the menu every day, paired with butter rolls so good they felt like a blessing. Walter's was just two doors down from 119 North Main.

If you counted the gas station, Drew had three places to get fried chicken. We didn't want to be the fourth. Les and I decided to open a sandwich shop instead, with a gift shop in the front. She'd handle the gift side. I'd take on the menu. It sounded simple enough.

Les went to market and turned the gift shop into something out of a magazine. She has a gift (if you'll pardon the pun). Pottery and pewter serving trays. Gourmet sauces and specialty martini olives. Candles that made the whole place smell amazing. It was kind of incredible, really.

While she curated beauty, I worked on the menu. Prosciutto, goat cheese, focaccia—ingredients that felt downright exotic in Drew.

I had no idea what I was doing. I read restaurant trade magazines and books on menu development. I studied what worked for others and tried to follow their lead. At night, Les and I would sit in bed—she'd scroll through her laptop looking for gift shop ideas, and I'd scribble down menu items.

By Christmas of 2004, Les had the gift shop stocked. The exact date slips my memory, but those early sales kept the lights on while I worked on the kitchen. The building was done, paid for with no debt. I used the equity to borrow $30,000 to buy gifts and equipment: fifty chairs, twelve tables, a sandwich cooler, a conveyor oven, a sink, a dishwasher, and just enough left over for our first food order. It was bare bones, but it was enough.

The food order came in on Thursday, the last day of April 2005. That night, we made everything on the menu for the first time. Susan Woods, my head line cook, was a trooper. She had some experience, but not with this menu. She learned it that night. We had a little party with friends and made only two of everything on the menu—sharing and talking up how good it was.

One night of training. That was it. By lunch on Friday, May 1, 2005, we were open. Looking back, I can't believe it. I'd written a menu, printed it, set an opening date, and never even tested the recipes. I was about to pay some Stupid Tax.

That soft opening wasn't soft at all. We got slammed. I learned a new phrase that day: "in the weeds." As a farmer, I knew exactly what that meant. Weeds are never good. The food crawled out of the kitchen. Nothing flowed. It was painfully obvious we weren't ready.

Our food rep, Lacy, jumped in to run the register. Les took her lunch break from work and ran food to tables. I turned into a delivery boy, promising to comp meals and bring them to folks who had to get back to their jobs.

The complaints poured in: slow service, no flow, chaos. But somehow, no one complained about the food. They liked it. They really liked it. That menu I'd dreamed up while sitting in bed actually worked.

We closed over the weekend to regroup—sat around licking our wounds and dissecting every misstep. Most of it boiled down to Susan needing more time to learn the menu. I hadn't given her enough training. I hadn't given anyone enough training. But there was no going back now. We were all in. We'd just have to figure it out on the fly.

I'd parachuted us in behind enemy lines with no plan and no preparation. Sink or swim. 119 North Main was now Main Street Deli & Gifts. And I was, for better or worse, in the restaurant business.

CHAPTER 19

The School of Hard Knocks

Ask any restaurant professional who they universally hate, and they'll tell you: it's the guy who opens a restaurant with no experience. I was that guy. I was the fool who looked at this business and thought, *That looks fun.*

People like me mess it all up for the serious ones in the room. I've seen it happen in farming, too. Some guy with no background shows up, jumps in the pool, and splashes water on everybody's towels. He knocks over drinks and drives up rents, messing with the bottom line of the neighbors who've been doing it for years. I get it. I probably looked like that guy at 119 North Main.

I wasn't taken seriously. I had no mentors, no guide. I learned the hard way—through trial and error. The people who knew better kept their distance, and I don't blame them.

The first few years weren't terrible, but they weren't good either. We made sales. Stayed busy. Sometimes it even felt like we had something. But the truth was, we didn't make money. Most months, we lost money. It was an expensive education, and I was a slow learner. The restaurant business is a brutal teacher. Even now, after all these years, I love the challenge.

About six months in, the Rebel Roost closed. I never asked if competition from me or Walter played a part in that. I don't know. Within a couple of years, Walter closed too—but he wasn't gone for good. He reopened out on Highway 49 a few years later, only to end up closing again. Even his building is gone now.

By then, I had hired Miss Jo Ann, Timbo's mom. She started bringing her magic into the kitchen. Fried ribs that made people sit back in their chairs and sigh. Pork steaks, fried and smothered in gravy—so tender you didn't need a knife. Those dishes weren't daily specials back then, but they made me realize we could be something different.

The gift shop was struggling even more than the restaurant. Les was stretched thin, juggling her full-time job at the dentist's office and a baby at home. Stafford Shurden Farms was growing, and my dad's health was failing. Cancer doesn't wait for anyone. The weight of 119 North Main was pressing on us from all sides. I was learning, but not fast enough. The restaurant was sinking. Thank goodness for the farm.

In 2006, I got an early start farming. I'd planted all my corn and most of my soybeans. It felt good to be ahead of the curve for once. On April 7, I was out planting food plots for ducks when I saw the cloud. It wasn't like other clouds. It was dark and strange, and it moved at a fast, ominous pace.

Before I could turn the tractor around, the wind hit. Then came the hail. It sounded like the windows of the cab were going to explode. Larry had left an old coat in the tractor, and I wrapped it around my head, bracing for the glass to shatter. It didn't.

And just like that, it was over. Larry was sitting in my truck nearby. The first thing I saw was the busted glass in the mirrors. Hail was everywhere. I could barely walk back to the truck. Then I noticed the grass along the road—it was gone. The leaves on the trees were stripped away. My crop wasn't just damaged. It was gone. Nothing but dirt remained.

In less than ten minutes, I had lost everything. I remembered that line from *Indiana Jones*: "Wiped clean by the hand of God." There was an eerie fog that rose as the ice melted against the warm Delta soil of Stafford Shurden Farms. I couldn't see.

The next day, I went out to look again. The damage was total. Every one of my farms had been hit. That night, as I sat in the wreckage of it all, Momma called. Daddy was gone. His fight was over.

In the span of twenty-four hours, I'd lost my best friend, my trusted mentor, and my crop. It felt like a punishment—like the universe had it out for me. I was crushed. It was the first time I'd ever really lost in this thing called life, and I didn't handle it well. It would take another loss, later in life, to finally set me right. I had been hit square in the face by life, and I was struggling.

CHAPTER 20

Judge Stafford Shurden

We buried my dad on a Tuesday. The next day, I was back in the field, replanting the crop we'd lost. Looking back, I know I needed to return to work that quickly. If it hadn't been for that hailstorm, I might not have. The storm forced me. Life has a way of doing that—pushing you forward when you don't want to move.

That same day, Barry Bryant came by 119 North Main. Barry was our local supervisor, and he needed to appoint someone to Dad's justice court judge position. He asked me. I didn't hesitate—I declined.

Barry wouldn't take no for an answer. He told me it was just until the special election—no strings attached, no expectation that I'd run. I agreed, reluctantly. The plan was to show up at the appointment meeting that next Monday and make it clear I wasn't running. But when Monday came, I stayed on the farm. Barry said he'd make the statement for me.

Later that day, Barry called. They'd decided not to include my statement in the minutes. They thought I should consider running. I didn't say no. By the end of the week, I was sworn in. Just like that, I became Judge Stafford Shurden.

I dove headfirst into the role. Unlike the restaurant business, where no one wanted to help, other judges reached out. Judge Pernell, my co-judge, took me under her wing. I sat with her in court and watched her work. Judges Straight and Ward over in Bolivar County became mentors. I tagged along like the little lost boy I was.

The court clerks were the real backbone. Angela Brenza in Indianola, and Susan Tackett and Helen Downs in Ruleville—they had decades of experience and kept me out of trouble. I could write a whole book about those years and the stories they produced.

Then there was the Mississippi Judicial College, founded by Judge Noah "Soggy" Sweat—a name that could only come from the humidity of Mississippi. Google his "Whiskey Speech" sometime. You'll thank me later. The Judicial College trained judges, especially non-lawyer judges like me. They reached out right after my appointment, and I leaned on them hard. Back then, I hated anything mandatory. Now, I miss those sessions. I've even gone back as a civilian to speak.

My first day in court as a judge was a mix of terror and excitement. My knees were shaking, but there was a spark I hadn't felt in a long time. It helped with the pain.

It didn't take long before I walked across the street to the courthouse and signed up to officially run for the position. I ordered yard signs and door hangers and started campaigning.

I have a big secret: I am shy. Very shy. I don't really like being put on the spot or speaking in public. Yet here I was, a judge. In court, when the judge speaks, everyone listens. On top of that, I was now knocking on strangers' doors and asking them for something. All of this was in complete conflict with the life I had known up to that point.

Don't get me wrong—once I start talking, you may have to punch me in the face to get me to stop. But flipping that switch takes some doing. I like being alone. I enjoy my time by myself on a tractor for sixteen hours. I can drive for hours with the radio off and just think.

I had a quick realization: I had to fake it until I made it. I had no confidence in April of 2006, but I knew that if I was going to knock on doors asking for votes, or sit on that bench and run a courtroom, people would want someone confident and in charge. I became that person because I had to.

One of the biggest lessons I learned from being a judge is that everyone feels like an impostor at the beginning—even the guy with the law degree I didn't have.

I was beginning to notice a theme in my life: starting things with no experience and being counted out early. My main opponent was Lemont Edwards—smart, polished, connected. His mom was the mayor of Ruleville, and his dad was the elected school superintendent of Sunflower County. No one thought I could win. They said I might make a runoff, maybe, thanks to a sympathy vote for my dad.

But I had no plans for a runoff. Dad had run against Lemont, and I had helped him. I had a general sense of where Dad's votes had come from. My plan was simple: outwork everyone. I was leaving no stone unturned.

My first day of door-knocking wasn't easy. I had my little door hangers, and I secretly hoped no one would be home so I could just leave a card and move on. I was so nervous. When a door opened, I'd lift my head, square my shoulders—good posture—and throw out my hand: "My name is Judge Stafford Shurden, and I would really appreciate your vote in November." I'd close with: "Lemont is a fine fella, but if he doesn't come by, I just want you to remember that I did." That pitch came from Charlie Capps, a legendary legislator and Dad's friend from Cleveland.

I had only made it about three blocks when I got a call from someone at one of the earlier houses. They knew and liked me, so they thought I'd want to know—my door card had a typo. The word *justice* was missing the "E." Here I was, running for justice court judge, and I couldn't even spell *justice*!

After correcting the cards, I kept canvassing—some areas I hit three times. In November, I won with almost 60 percent of the vote. Lemont became a good friend. I don't see him often, but when we do run into each other, we always talk for a while.

I ran for judge three more times. In my last election, I received 84.75 percent of the total votes in Sunflower County, Mississippi. I was proud of that. In my hometown of Drew, I got nearly 93 percent. That's an insane number, and I was blessed by the people of Drew for it.

I learned a lot from being a judge, and in many ways, it made me a better man. Over time, I grew more confident and understood how and when to insert myself. I saw the same problems repeat themselves—just different faces and bodies. But they were the same mistakes. Both failure and success leave clues.

I learned how to read people. I learned how to motivate people—and what motivates them. I have many friends today who started out in front of me, receiving jail time. But above all, I learned how to listen. Real listening. Not just staying quiet, but paying close attention to what's said and what's not. I think today, I understand people better. That's helped me in every aspect of life. I learned how to connect with people, even on their worst day.

In the end, being a judge ran its course. I had hit the ceiling from day one—no upward mobility as a non-lawyer judge. And frankly, it wasn't in my nature. Most of the time, I made people mad. That just came with the job. I upset both criminals and law enforcement. Sometimes it was because I was wrong. Judges are people too. We make mistakes. To those I wronged, I'm truly sorry. I also believe—strongly—that no one should hold an elected position for life. Term limits are good.

After my last election, I wrote a letter to the editor expressing my concerns about government and politics in general. In it, I declared I wouldn't run again. I painted myself into a corner, so if I ever changed my mind, I'd look foolish.

I carry a great deal of wisdom from my years as a judge, and I'm deeply thankful for that time. The skills I developed while presiding as a judge continue to serve me well every single day. Being Judge Shurden was a laboratory in human nature.

That said, I'm also very glad I'm no longer in politics—and, as a rule, I don't talk about politics. I've done my civic duty and served. If you're curious to understand more deeply why I feel this way, I encourage you to read George Washington's Farewell Address. It remains one of the most important political documents ever written—and it's still just as relevant today.

CHAPTER 21

Autopilot

I was farming 2,500 acres in the Mississippi Delta. I was the justice court judge for Sunflower County and the municipal judge for the City of Ruleville. I owned a restaurant at 119 North Main in Drew. And now, I was also a father to two baby girls, Mary Stafford and Anna Walton, and a husband to Les. Life had become a delicate balancing act, teetering between accomplishment and exhaustion.

After my dad passed, my mom took it harder than I did. Grief settled in her like the Delta fog—heavy and unrelenting. The house, the church pew, the corner table at the country club—they were all reminders of her life with my dad. There were just too many ghosts in Drew. So, just before Anna Walton was born, Mom packed up her life and moved to Madison. She had always dreamed of a bigger town, and Madison had everything Drew didn't: safety, amenities, and a chance to start anew.

Les and I made a decision then. We sold the house we'd just bought in town and moved into the home I grew up in—a ranch-style place at the end of A. W. Shurden Road, surrounded by four acres. I wanted my daughters to know that yard the way I had—full of barefoot summers and endless possibilities. Here, there were no random cars for them to be wary of. Here, they had quiet freedom.

Les got to work making the house her own. She remodeled the kitchen, whitewashed the pecky cypress in the den, and brightened the long, dark hallway with fresh paint. Little by little, she transformed my childhood memories into a home for our family.

Les cooked a lot in our new home, too. She makes chicken and dumplings like Mammy used to. The house was remodeled, but our little family was having dinner each night in just about the same spot as when I was a kid. I needed that.

They needed me. But I was working too hard. Spreading myself too thin—judge, farmer, restaurateur, husband, father. I was good at most of it, most of the time. And I was failing at all of it, some of the time.

The truth about those years is complicated. There were bright moments, like the family vacations Les and I took with the girls—journeys I wouldn't trade for the world. But behind the smiles and snapshots, the restaurant was bleeding money. The farm, for a while, outpaced the losses, and the steady paychecks from my two judgeships gave me a false sense of security. It was enough to keep me from seeing the truth: one bad crop, and everything would collapse. It was a house of cards, and I had built it.

Farming is a beautiful thing. There's therapy in being tethered to the land, in watching the seasons turn and feeling yourself part of something eternal. But farming is also brutal. Winter always comes—in farming and in life, both literally and figuratively.

In 2014, winter hit hard. The worst crop I'd ever grown came just as crop prices dropped thirty percent. The restaurant went through its first identity crisis, changing its name from Main Street Deli and Gifts to Stafford's on Main. I was borrowing a hundred grand a month just to stay afloat.

Perhaps the only good change in my professional life came at the restaurant. 119 North Main was now serving the meat and three meals of my youth, and I was going to need that comfort.

The storm clouds of winter were gathering, and I was running on autopilot. Distracted. Unprepared.

PART III

Setting the Table

CHAPTER 22

1933

Just a year earlier, I was strapped for cash in both businesses. I made a very conscious decision: if I was going down, I was going down fighting. I decided it was time to expand my restaurant experience into a larger market. After more than a decade in the business, I felt confident that I finally knew enough to make that move.

I first explored nearby Clarksdale and even met with Bill Luckett about renting the shuttered restaurant he and Morgan Freeman had owned. Madidi's was a high-end restaurant designed to complement their Ground Zero Blues Club, but it ended up requiring more management than either of them wanted to commit. So, they closed it. I think today it's been converted into upscale apartments.

Around that time, Billy Marlow from Ruleville heard I was looking and invited me to scout for potential locations there. Ruleville, under Billy's leadership, had become a small economic powerhouse—but it was just four miles from Drew. I was planning to open another "Stafford's-style" lunch place, and that proximity made it impractical. Besides, Billy didn't want a lunch spot. What he wanted was a fine dining venue where he could entertain and impress guests for the hospital he ran—a very political business, as it turns out. Billy correctly reasoned that they needed a place with a wow factor.

About a month after our meeting, my friend, Stacy, called to say we were about to break ground on the renovation. I was as surprised as anyone. I asked her to pause and arranged another meeting with Billy.

The building was owned by the nonprofit arm of the hospital, which had the funds to renovate it and lease it to me on a deal that was frankly too good to pass up. I had no idea how to operate a high-end steak and seafood place, but with a small, easily secured loan for equipment, we were off.

The renovation was... interesting. There was no blueprint, just Stacy and me improvising as we went, mostly Stacy, with me playing the role of brakes. Stacy has impeccable high-end taste, so I knew the place would look more like New York than Ruleville. One day, I walked in to find workers upstairs cutting a hole in the roof. Stacy was directing. She had woken up that morning and decided a skylight would be perfect for the upstairs bar—and it was.

I had also come up with a concept I still love to this day: a Prohibition-era steak and seafood restaurant with a New Orleans flair, focused on period cocktails and rich Southern flavors. We named it 1933 Restaurant & Bar, after the final year of Prohibition. What followed was a chapter straight out of a Bourdain book—and I was not prepared.

I had read *Kitchen Confidential*, but I still had no idea what I was stepping into. The drinking, drug use, casual sex, fights, and good old-fashioned debauchery Bourdain described turned out to be just the tip of the iceberg. I won't lie—it was a lot of fun, even though I personally didn't participate in most of it.

As the renovation progressed under Stacy's guidance, I began building the team. First, I poached Cody from a local food purveyor to be our chef. He brought along Hobbit as his sous chef. Then I hired possibly the best bartender in the entire country, Kevin. Both Cody and Kevin deserve books of their own.

Kevin was a force of nature—the kind of person you couldn't ignore even if you tried. A true master of his craft, he was a cocktail savant at a time when I, a man who rarely drank, was opening a bar built around craft cocktails. Kevin became the teacher; I was the student. He taught me the alchemy of spirits and mixers—what pairs with which juice, what to shake, what to stir. Because, as I learned, yes—you can bruise a cocktail.

Kevin's reputation preceded him. People would walk into the bar and confidently say, "Just have Kevin make me something." And Kevin, in his signature style, would slyly ask, "What don't you like?" If they said gin, you could bet your ass they were getting gin—and they'd love it. That was Kevin's magic.

Long before it was trendy, Kevin was taking cheap liquor and transforming it into something elevated using mason jars and fresh ingredients. Cucumber vodka, strawberry tequila—his infusions lined the bar wall like trophies. His masterpiece? A blanco tequila infused with strawberry and jalapeño. My friends, let me tell you: that was the best margarita I've ever had. Sweet up front with a little tickle of jalapeño on the back end. Kevin even had us making all our mixers from scratch—squeezing limes and lemons one by one behind the bar every day before service.

At the time, Kevin was in his thirties. As brilliant as he was behind the bar, he was a walking disaster in real life. He had his payroll deposited directly into his father's account because his dad had to ration out his money. This same grown man once managed to wreck three cars in one week. After the third wreck, his dad stormed into the restaurant before service, red-faced and ready to throttle him. I saw him coming, stepped outside, and ran interference—convinced this was the day Kevin was going to meet his maker. I slowed him down just enough to keep him from committing filicide.

Kevin lived on the edge, and I bailed him out more times than I can count—out of jail, out of fights with angry husbands, out of hangovers so brutal he could barely stand. I fed him coffee, sobered him up just enough to make it through a shift. I threatened to kill him myself more than once—and at the time, I meant it. But Kevin had this gift with people. Guests would come in ready to wring his neck and leave as his biggest fans.

One night, I watched Kevin do the impossible. A *two-top*—restaurant lingo for a table of two—of notorious "no-tippers" came in on a particularly busy night. Nobody wanted to serve them. They were nice people, but they never tipped. Kevin just said, "I got this, boss." He juggled the entire bar while taking care of the couple. They tipped him fifty bucks. Fifty. Bucks. Kevin could charm anyone—even the impossible ones.

As I write this, I feel that same mix of frustration and admiration I always felt for Kevin. I cannot count the number of times I wanted to hold his head underwater, just for a minute. But if I had a liquor license, I'd hire him back today. No question. His talent is nearly divine.

Kevin is a gift—a hurricane of chaos and genius. And despite every headache he caused, I'd break all my rules to have him on my team again.

Because when Kevin's in the room, there's nobody better at what he does. Nobody.

Now Cody—Cody is a big guy. The kind who looks more like a bouncer than a chef. A mountain of a man with a grin that says he's definitely up to something. He's the type who runs toward a fight, laughing the whole way, fueled by adrenaline and a deep love of chaos. Swearing was his second language, and he spoke it fluently, slinging expletives at everyone with an affection only Cody could get away with. And let's not forget his love for practical jokes, most of which went way too far.

Like the time Cody thought it'd be hilarious to change a server's name in the system to that word—the C-word for a certain part of the female anatomy. Harmless enough, he thought, until it started printing on customer receipts. Most people didn't notice, but one lady did—and she was livid. She was convinced the insult was aimed directly at her, and honestly, I couldn't blame her. I got the call, and I was furious. Cody swore it was a joke gone wrong. I told him point-blank: his job depended on fixing it.

Years later, Cody confessed he had to mute his mic during that phone call because he was laughing so hard. Laughing in my face. But somehow, the man walked into that firestorm and worked his magic. He had that customer laughing along with him. Think about that for a second—Cody essentially called her that word and still charmed his way out of it. That's Cody for you.

As wild as he was, Cody was a damn good chef. The man could cook like his life depended on it. He worked hard, cared deeply, and created food that blew people away. Maybe there was a little alcohol—or even something else—in the mix, but I never knew it, and it never got in the way. What ultimately did him in at 1933 were his antics. Cody knows it, and that's one of the things I respect about him: he owns his chaos.

We're still friends to this day, and if I ever needed him at Stafford's, I know he'd show up in a heartbeat, ready to jump in and work like nothing ever happened. Cody is one of a kind: equal parts maddening and brilliant. The world's a lot more interesting with him in it.

Cody's replacement was a chef I'll call "Big Cat." Big Cat was an exceptional chef. His food was outstanding, and he had a gift for the kind of comfort food I loved. Even in our high-end steak and seafood restaurant, he'd serve meatloaf on a cold Saturday night—and I respected that about him.

Big Cat had been in the Marines, but he was kicked out. I never asked why, and he never offered the story. He had a big heart—and an equally big appetite for Kentucky Tavern, or KT, as he called it. I never saw him do drugs, but I'd heard rumors. I was even told the dishwasher was selling Coke to the crew, but I could never prove it.

Big Cat had a temper. Occasionally, he would quit in the middle of service, only to return before I even knew he was gone. He understood that I didn't have the patience for that kind of drama. Still, despite his flaws, Big Cat stuck with us until the very last day. When I told him we were closing, he felt responsible. He wasn't—but that was the kind of man he was. He cared deeply about the food and the people. I loved that guy.

A couple of years after 1933 closed, Big Cat called me. He was going through a rough divorce, and it hit him hard. We talked about getting him into a twelve-step program, and he genuinely wanted to try. I prayed for him to succeed.

Not long after, Big Cat passed away in his sleep on a friend's couch. I've never asked what really happened, and I don't want to know.

His funeral took place during COVID, and it was packed. All these hard-edged restaurant people were there, hugging, grieving, mourning the loss of our friend. In the restaurant world, we may be competitors, but we're also a tight-knit tribe. Losing him was tough.

*****

Wednesdays at 1933 were special. We called it "Wine Down Wednesday," featuring wine and oyster specials with live music. It turned Ruleville into a midweek destination. Working with those bands made me realize how similar musicians and kitchen staff are: both love food and music, both work odd hours, both have their share of groupies, and both sometimes indulge in the darker side of nightlife.

I remember one musician asking me—a sitting judge at the time—to leave a line of coke on the urinal so his girlfriend wouldn't find out. When I refused, he asked for a shot of tequila instead, also to be left on the urinal. I refused again, but I'm pretty sure Kevin or someone else helped him out, because later I found empty shot glasses in the men's bathroom.

I tried hiring a manager at 1933, but they never lasted long. In the final year, I managed the restaurant myself, even collaborating with Big Cat to change the menu weekly. It was fun, but it was too much. Mary Stafford was in eleventh grade, and I was missing everything. I wanted to be more present in her life—and her sister's. Our food was excellent, but the restaurant wasn't making enough money, and the farm was losing ground. I became terrified of insolvency. I didn't want 1933 to become one of those restaurants where employees show up to a locked door and a note—a thing that happens all too often in this industry.

Three years after opening, I called a meeting and told the staff we'd be closing in two months. We shut down on our own terms, with all bills paid and every staff member lined up with a new job before the doors closed. Every single one of them stayed and worked until the final day.

I learned so much from that experience. The food and drinks were great, but that wasn't enough. I was a poor manager and owner. I had no standard operating procedures. I tried to do too much myself instead of delegating. I didn't manage cash flow properly. The truth is, any restaurant that fails has one core problem: the owner. I was the problem. I allowed those after-hours scenes to get out of hand. I chose the location. I chose the name. I tolerated tardiness. I hired the people. Me. It was me.

Today, my friend, Dennis Cheshire, runs The Pharm in that location, and he does a fantastic job. It's still strange to eat there and not be running plates or hustling cash to pay the band, but The Pharm is a great place, and Dennis is a great guy. I recommend it.

CHAPTER 23

"A Man Ain't Nothing if He Ain't Got Land"—Oh Brother, Where Art Thou

Oh, how I wish I didn't have to write this chapter. It's embarrassing. Hard. I hate thinking about it, let alone putting it down in words. But this is my story, so I feel compelled to tell it.

After the farming debacle of 2014, I was drowning in debt—millions owed to Planters Bank and Sanders Seed Co., a small seed and chemical supplier out of Cleveland. On paper, I wasn't bankrupt; I had equity—land, equipment, and other assets I'd accumulated over years of farming. But the numbers didn't lie: I couldn't cash flow. I had more assets than debt, yet I couldn't make the payments. That cold, hard lesson didn't make sense to me until it hit me square in the face.

In December, I went to both Planters and Sanders with a plan—a way to restructure the debt and move forward, much like my dad had done in 1969. His fix took one year. Mine would take several, and I'd need to change how I ran both the farm and the restaurant. To their credit, they agreed.

The following year was good. A great crop, a season full of promise. I paid what I'd committed to, and things started to feel like they were turning around. Then Sanders was sold to a larger company. The new owners didn't care about the handshake agreement I'd made with the old ones. They wanted full payment—immediately. No compromises. I couldn't pay, so they sued me.

Let me be clear: I wasn't happy with them, but I can admit I'd done a poor job communicating. I owed the money, fair and square. Still, when the papers were served, it felt like a punch to the gut. I called Planters Bank to let them know, then went straight to a lawyer.

I asked him to make a deal with both parties. I was willing to sell a piece of land I'd bought in 2005 to pay them off if they'd drop the suit. But we couldn't reach an agreement. So I filed for Chapter 12 bankruptcy. It's a protection specifically designed for farmers, meant to restructure debt, not erase it. My goal wasn't to escape what I owed, but to ensure I didn't lose everything in a fire sale.

Looking back, I know I panicked. The fear of being sued—the weight of it all—got to me. In hindsight, I wish I hadn't filed. We made several good crops in a row after that, and I could've stayed the course, paid everyone back, and kept my land. But I didn't know that then.

Being sued is terrifying. It makes you feel small and cornered. I overreacted, and I still feel the repercussions of that decision today. Both Planters and Sanders were eventually paid more than they probably expected. I held on to the farming business and 119 North Main, but the cost was real.

Through it all, I made one good decision in a sea of bad ones: I insisted on dealing with my creditors directly whenever possible. Normally, bankruptcy lawyers send out letters saying, *"Don't contact my client."* But I didn't want that. I wanted to look them in the eye. I felt no one could explain my situation better than me, and I didn't want to be seen as the guy hiding behind an attorney. It turned out to be the best call I made. Today, I still do business with those same people, and the relationships are strong.

I sold my land to a good man named Jeb Bridges. He leased it back to me, and we've become friends. It's a strange comfort to be farming that land now as a tenant. There are days when I'm out there, looking over the fields, and I feel a quiet sting. That land slipped through my fingers. I let it go.

Thank God my mom still owns what my dad left her. That's something.

As painful as it all was, the bankruptcy forced me to pay closer attention to my numbers, both on the farm and at the restaurant. We closed 1933 and sold a lot of things, but we survived. I'm a better businessman because of it. I am generally a never-look-back type of person. I don't dwell. I am very good at just picking up and moving on, but sometimes, late at night, I think about the land I lost. It feels like a scar I'll carry forever.

CHAPTER 24

Restaurant Makeover

There's nothing quite like fear to shake you awake. At 119 North Main, fear lived in the walls—pressed into the wood grain of the counter, breathing alongside the hiss of the fryer. Stafford's wasn't just a restaurant. It was like a family member you keep sending to rehab who keeps relapsing. You never give up on family… until you do. I didn't want to give up, but Stafford's was bleeding money. I couldn't let it fail—not just for me, but for the people who depended on it.

Stafford's, as 119 North Main had come to be known, had become a stalwart in the community. A cornerstone. A place where the moments that knit a town together unfolded. After hours, baby showers filled the dining room with laughter and pastel decorations. On Friday nights, wedding rehearsals brought the promise of new beginnings, and senior parties for the high school lit up the space with youthful energy and bittersweet goodbyes. This wasn't just a business anymore—it was the heart of Drew. The last thing left. Stafford's wasn't just a location; it was the meeting place, the glue that held the community together.

Drew, Mississippi, didn't even have a grocery store anymore. For some, Stafford's was the only place they'd get a square meal all day. People like

Mr. Buddy Tuck Miller. A retired farmer, a widower, a man of quiet humor and dignity—he showed up every day like clockwork. Bryce, who's been with Stafford's for over a decade now, and the girls behind the counter doted on him. They called him "Mr. Buddy," asked how he was doing every single day, and every single day, he'd grin and say, "I'm up and taking nourishment."

When it came time to order, his answer was always the same: "Fish heads and rice." He'd say it with a sparkle in his eye and a boyish grin—not bad for a man in his eighties—knowing full well that wasn't on the menu. Mr. Buddy had roots in this place. He owned Promised Land Farm, the namesake of our most popular dish, the Promised Land Croissant. His son, Tucker, was one of my Uncle Reggie's best friends and took me on my first duck hunt. Tucker and I still sing in the church choir together.

Mr. Buddy's gone now, but when I think about the people we served at Stafford's, he's the one I see most clearly. He loved us, and we loved him. Folks like him deserved to be cared for—to have a place where someone remembered their name, their stories, and their preferences. That thought, along with the image of my daughters, kept me up at night, strategizing how to save this place.

Mary Stafford grew up on 119 North Main. By sixth grade, she was waiting tables, her bright smile lighting up the dining room. She had a streak of rebellion, though. When I bought her a side-by-side ATV, I told her to drive through the alley to avoid stirring up trouble in town. I didn't want people saying the judge's daughter got special treatment. Naturally, she'd roar straight down Main Street and park right in front of the restaurant, claiming, "The chief says it's fine." She knew him as a customer, of course.

Anna Walton, my youngest, didn't know life without a restaurant. She was born into a world of clattering dishes and the steady hum of conversation. At three years old, she'd walk around with a pen and pad, pretending to take orders. By the time she was old enough to actually work, her creative spark found its way into the kitchen. She loves to bake at home, and her summers are spent at Stafford's, tying her identity to the rhythm of the restaurant.

But none of that mattered if I couldn't keep the doors open.

I took a hard look at our operation. The food was good, but that wasn't enough. Revenue was the real problem. Drew's population couldn't sustain us. We needed a bigger net. I had to either bring people to us or take our food to them.

Catering became our lifeline. By 2019, it accounted for nearly 40 percent of our revenue. Some days, I was up before dawn, cooking for fifty to a hundred people, loading it all into my truck, and driving across North Mississippi—Oxford, Tupelo, Southaven, Clarksdale, Greenville, and more. I was taking meat and three to the state, one buffet line at a time.

The best part was that my overhead barely changed. Food costs were the only real expense. The labor was mostly just me. For the first time, the restaurant paid me. For the first time, I saw a way forward.

I thought I'd cracked the code. I thought we were safe. But in this business, you learn quickly: there's always another storm on the horizon.

CHAPTER 25

A Social World

When I opened my restaurant at 119 North Main in 2005, I had no idea how much the world would change in the years to come. In 2006, I ran for judge, making my first foray into public life. Both of these milestones came before the iPhone revolutionized the world in 2007. Back then, social media existed, but smartphones put it in everyone's pocket—and that changed everything.

I remember laughing at text messaging when it first started. Now, I'd much rather receive a text than a call. I even swore I'd never have a Facebook account. On the day we opened the restaurant, we didn't even accept debit cards—and now we take Apple Pay!

It's funny to think about now: if the smartphone were a person, it still wouldn't be old enough to drink in the US. These are still very young technologies, but in a short time, they've completely transformed how we live, work, and connect. I laughed at texting. I laughed at smartphones. I laughed at social media. And I was so wrong. These tools have reshaped the game entirely, and I've adapted well.

In 2013, I read *Jab, Jab, Jab, Right Hook* by Gary Vaynerchuk, and it clicked. That book opened my eyes to the potential of social media. I vowed never to be a slow adopter again. By my final campaign for judge, I had embraced it fully. In 2006, I spent $15,000 of my own money on traditional media. For my last election, I spent nothing on it, relying entirely on social media. I won with 83.75 percent of the vote in Sunflower County.

Part of that shift wasn't just philosophical—it was practical. I was broke. I didn't have money for ads or fancy campaigns. All I had was determination, a good pair of walking shoes, and a free tool: social media.

Early in the campaign, I called my former opponent, Lemont Edwards, and asked if I could put a sign in his yard. He graciously said yes. I snapped a picture of that sign, posted it with a message of gratitude—and the post went viral. That moment created a wave of momentum I never lost. I owe you, Lemont!

After the election, life knocked me down. Bankruptcy, the closing of 1933, and the sale of land weighed heavily on me. Searching for direction, I turned to books and motivational events, even attending a Tony Robbins seminar. Most mornings, I'd walk around town, reflecting on the mess I'd made and trying to find a way forward.

One day, I decided to film my thoughts and post them to my social media page. It *wasn't* more for myself than for anyone else. I figured if I was struggling, maybe someone else was too.

That first video didn't get many views, but the feedback was immediate. People stopped me in grocery stores and at football games to thank me.

They told me I had given them hope. So, I kept posting. Slowly but surely, my following grew.

For Stafford's and 1933, we began heavily using social media. Live streaming was new, and it became a priority. And it worked. Just like my campaign, we didn't have much of a marketing budget, but social media gave us a direct line to customers. As our online presence grew, so did our sales. The proof was undeniable.

I got so good at managing our social media that people would ask which firm we had hired. At 1933, I drove so much business that our staff struggled to keep up. It was a good problem to have, but it also exposed gaps in my leadership. I was great at marketing, but I was still learning how to build a team and establish systems. The reality was, I had been holding back on marketing because I knew our operations couldn't handle the volume. Leadership became my next frontier.

Social media and the internet have become virtually synonymous. Much like when television took over from radio, businesses have had to adapt. Early TV ads were essentially radio spots with a picture. Similarly, many people still treat social media as a one-way broadcast. But social media demands authenticity. It's not just about talking at someone—it's about engaging with them.

Today's customers expect businesses to be responsive and genuine. If you're not on social media, people assume you're closed. It's the modern-day equivalent of not answering the phone. Social media allows businesses to build real connections with their clients and the public at large. That two-way conversation is a game changer for someone like me who thrives on connection.

But authenticity comes with risk. One wrong move can spiral into a PR disaster. Chrysler learned this the hard way in 2011 when someone accidentally tweeted a profanity-laced rant about Detroit drivers from the company's official account. DiGiorno stumbled in 2014, posting a tone-deaf comment using a hashtag intended to support survivors of domestic violence. And who could forget the American Apparel intern who mistakenly posted an image of the Challenger explosion, thinking it was fireworks?

Most recently, a restaurant in south Mississippi—whose name I'll withhold—went viral for all the wrong reasons after a drunken political tirade was posted online. One of the owners appeared to be in their underwear.

These are cautionary tales. Social media is powerful, but it's not a toy. Misuse it, and you can create a disaster faster than a drunk Mississippi Delta boy biting into a bad piece of fried chicken. If you don't have the time or the expertise to manage it well, hire someone who does.

For years, I navigated the tricky balance of being both a judge and a social media advocate. The role came with restrictions, and the Code of Judicial Conduct required a certain level of restraint—even online. I couldn't fully unleash my creativity, but I learned to work within those limits.

When my time as judge ended in 2019, I was ready to take the brakes off. My businesses were doing much better, and I had grown as a leader. I knew 2020 would be our year. Of course, none of us saw what was coming.

If you're diving into social media for your business, tread carefully. It's one of the most powerful tools in your arsenal—but also one of the most dangerous. The key is authenticity. Show your customers who you are, engage with them, and give them a reason to connect. Social media isn't just about selling—it's about building relationships and fostering connection. And in today's world, that means everything.

CHAPTER 26

2020

It feels fitting to give the year 2020 its own chapter. It was the year when everything changed, and nothing would ever be the same. In our household, we often divide our personal history on this blue sphere into two eras: pre-COVID and post-COVID. For anyone reading this, I don't need to explain the masks, the deaths, or the fear that settled in around March of that year. You already know.

But January of 2020 felt different. For the first time in over a decade, I wasn't tethered to the role of *judge*. That chapter of my life had closed, and I was ready to push Stafford's Market to new heights. The restaurant was turning a profit, thanks to a booming catering business. We had landed a big contract with the State of Mississippi and were delivering lunches to nearly every medical clinic in the area. It felt like things were finally falling into place.

With the limitations of being a judge behind me, my team and I started brainstorming ways to take full advantage of social media. We talked about doing something like Dave Portnoy's pizza reviews—but with fried chicken. We figured if I became the go-to authority on fried chicken, people would naturally assume ours was the best. We made a list of all the top fried chicken spots we could think of—and aside from Gus's in Memphis, they were all gas stations. That realization made me laugh at first, but the more I thought about it, the more it made sense.

Gas station food in Mississippi is wildly underrated. Over the years, we'd hosted plenty of food writers at our restaurants, many of whom were touring the Delta in search of hidden gems. Almost all of them were fascinated by our gas station food culture. In big cities, chefs unwind after their shifts at bars with great food. In rural Mississippi, there are no late-night bars with gourmet snacks—our chefs head to all-night gas stations.

The idea of reviewing gas station food lingered, but it wasn't until late January that it finally came to life. My daughter, Anna Walton, and I were heading to Indianola to renew my tag when the conversation turned to fried chicken livers. She admitted she'd never tried them. We stopped at Double Quick #1 and picked up fried chicken and chicken livers. In a moment that can only be described as hubris mixed with serendipity, I let down the tailgate to use as a table, and *Gas Station Tailgate Review* was born.

That first video was raw. I edited it with Windows Movie Maker and posted it online. Friends called me, laughing, asking what the hell I was doing. But the video went viral. So I made another. And then another. By the time I was invited onto Rebecca Turner's syndicated radio show, *What's Good, Mississippi?*, the videos had taken on a life of their own. Rebecca asked how long I'd been doing it, thinking it had been a few years. "Three weeks," I said, and we both laughed.

At first, my style mimicked Portnoy's. I cracked jokes, especially when the food was bad—those videos always got the most views. By spring break, I had reviewed every local spot I could think of, so we planned a family trip to the Gulf Coast and New Orleans, hitting places along the way. We stopped at Rose's BBQ in Hattiesburg and Bradley's Cajun Quick Stop in Long Beach. The plan was to keep filming.

But as we drove to New Orleans, everything changed. Every radio station was reporting on COVID-19. It had gone from a whisper to the only thing anyone was talking about. In the span of that one-hour drive, every catering event we had booked was canceled. Every single one. Our cash cow had been unceremoniously slaughtered—and we hadn't even made it to New Orleans yet.

At the hotel, we overheard a man checking out. His cruise had been canceled. That's when it hit me. This wasn't just a localized overreaction. This was real. The next morning, we packed up and headed home.

When we got back, the world was shutting down. Restaurant dining rooms were ordered to close. Catering completely evaporated with COVID restrictions and wouldn't come back in full for more than two years, and dine-in service was also off the table, at least for a while. We were in full-blown crisis mode. We pivoted so hard, we even changed the name of 119 North Main from Stafford's on Main to Stafford's Market, reflecting our new approach. We sold anything people were willing to buy—family meals, ready-to-cook dinners, and, of course, toilet paper. We didn't have a drive-through, so we offered curbside service: just pull up front, call in your order, and we'd bring the food out.

Mary Stafford, home from college, began delivering meals to shut-ins, leaving food on porches and retrieving payment from envelopes in mailboxes. She became a familiar sight in her little black Acura—the food car, as hospital security called it. They were hesitant to let her onto the hospital campus at first because of the restrictions, but before long, they were waving her through with gratitude to feed workers that didn't have access to the hospital cafeteria.

With me doing most of the cooking during COVID, I decided to double down on our meat and three offerings. We simplified the menu to feature just one daily meat and three and a couple of sandwiches. This shift was partly due to the logistical challenges of the pandemic, but we quickly realized people were craving the comfort of a home-cooked meal. That sense of familiarity and warmth resonated deeply with our customers. Even now, the trend toward comfort food continues. What's fascinating is seeing young people—many of whom didn't grow up with this style of cooking—find their own sense of nostalgia in it. It's a reminder that some things, like good, simple food, transcend time.

That time I spent in the kitchen during COVID forever changed the way I think about both food and the restaurant business.

The gas station reviews stopped, of course. "Two weeks to flatten the curve," they told us. Two weeks turned into months. Somewhere in that haze of survival, I realized I wasn't the only one hurting. We all were. But restaurants were taking the brunt of it. I picked up my camera again—not just for me, but for everyone fighting to keep their doors open.

One of my first reviews after the restart was at United Deli in Columbus, Mississippi. I met the owner, John, and ordered the John Special Sandwich. It was supposed to be six inches, but I measured it on camera—thirteen inches. John's wife baked the bread herself, cutting it before it rose. That sandwich was incredible, and the video exploded online. Fifty thousand views in no time. John later sent word through a food supplier that the video had really helped his business.

That knowledge changed me. From that point on, I made a vow: no more negative reviews. If the food was bad, I'd pack up and move on to the next spot. My mission was to shine a light on the people fighting to survive and putting in good work, just like me.

As the year wore on, I got a call from a guy named Wright Thompson. He was working on a story for *The Atlantic* about Emmett Till and had questions about my family. I was reluctant at first, but we became fast friends. Wright's book, *Pappyland,* was about to come out, and he joined me on *Gas Station Tailgate Review* to promote it. He even connected me with a producer at ESPN's SEC Network about doing a segment for their gameday show. It never panned out, but I'll always be grateful for his support. That story for *The Atlantic* ended up becoming a multiyear rabbit hole and eventually turned into Wright's bestselling book, *The Barn*. It's a heavy read, but well worth it.

By the end of 2020, we had survived. None of the team at Stafford's ever got COVID. The restaurant was holding its own, the farm had produced a great crop, and some semblance of normalcy had begun to return. For all the loss and chaos of that year, I'll always cherish the quiet nights at home with my wife and daughters, watching *Stranger Things* and finding comfort in each other. Even in the hardest times, there's something beautiful to hold onto.

As my friend Robert St. John says, *"onward."*

CHAPTER 27

Summer Rain

The year 2021 began with promise. Life felt lighter, as if the worst of the storm had passed. We hired a new chef at 119 North Main, and the dining room was open again. The shadow of bankruptcy that had loomed over me for years was now just that—a shadow. COVID was beginning to shrink into the rearview mirror, and for the first time in a long time, life was starting to feel normal.

Shurden Farms was a very different operation by then. What had once been a sprawling 3,000-acre farm with a full team of employees and equipment had been pared down to less than 1,000 acres. It was just me now. Spot, my sprayer man, had fallen ill and was on benefits. Blackbird, in his late sixties, had retired, as had Isack, the best driver I'd ever known. It was just me and the land. And truth be told, I was enjoying the solitude.

There's a certain pride in working the land alone. The glass of a John Deere tractor cab became my office window, just as it had been in my youth, and the rhythmic hum of the engine provided the soundtrack to my days. Planting the crop was a solitary kind of joy. I could get that part done in about seven days, with precision and purpose. I figured harvest would be the same. With the restaurant running smoothly under the new chef and catering still not fully back, I had time to focus on the farm and *Gas Station Tailgate Review*.

By May, I was feeling optimistic. The crop had the prettiest start I'd ever seen, and the farm was lean, efficient, and had the potential to be profitable. One more good year, and I'd have money in the bank again. Things were looking up.

One evening that May, I was scrolling through Instagram and saw an event announcement for *Ben's Book Club*. Wright Thompson and Ben Napier were hosting an event in Laurel, Mississippi, to promote Wright's book, *Pappyland*. Tickets weren't cheap, but I didn't hesitate. Ben and his wife, Erin, had done incredible work revitalizing Laurel through their HGTV show *Home Town*. I'd never watched the show, but I admired their impact on our state. Always a cheerleader for Mississippi, I wanted to see their work firsthand, and I wanted to support my friend, Wright.

The event was set for mid-June. As the date approached, the weather had been dry, and I figured I'd need to start watering the soybeans soon. I was starting to think I might be working the day of the event in Laurel. Rain was in the forecast for June 7, but never came. I was not happy that day. The next morning, the sky finally opened up, and in about an hour, we got what we needed. I felt relieved. The radar showed a narrow band of storms, stretching from Pace, Mississippi, near the Mississippi River, to Charleston, Mississippi at the bluff hills—and my farm sat right in the middle of it.

Then it kept raining. And raining. And raining. By the end of June 8, we'd gotten nine inches. All night and the next day, the storm refused to move. It was like a train running over the same stretch of track, hammering the same narrow swath of land. Highway 49 was closed, as was Highway 32. Drew, just seven miles south, saw homes in low-lying areas flooded. Boats were dispatched to take the elderly to safety. I could see the boats from the window of 119 North Main. At least that was high ground.

By June 10, water started seeping through the cracks in the floor at 119 North Main. We closed the restaurant that day. I drove to Walmart and bought a wet-dry vac, thinking I could stay ahead of it. By the time I got back, the rains had started to recede, but it was too late. In just seventy-two hours, Drew had been hit with eighteen inches of rain. Shurden Farms, seven miles north, had gotten twenty-four. It was Biblical.

There was no going to the farm. The roads were impassable. It was nearly a week before I could see the damage in person. A friend had flown a drone over the fields and sent me the footage. It looked like the ocean, with nothing but trees poking through the water. Every crop, every seed I'd planted, was gone. Farms to the south—spared from the rain—lost some of their crops too when the Quiver and Sunflower Rivers overflowed their banks. The old-timers who gathered at the restaurant said they'd never seen anything like it. They called it a hundred-year event, and I hope they're right.

Despite the devastation, I decided to go to Ben's Book Club. I didn't tell Wright I was coming. When the event began, they were giving away bottles of Maker's Mark bourbon, and Wright spotted me in the crowd. "There's a man who needs this more than anyone," he said, calling me to the front and explaining the flood. To my surprise, no one there had even heard about it. Mississippi had moved on, but Shurden Farms hadn't.

That night, I met Ben Napier, and we hit it off right away. He's one of the best people I've ever met, and I'm proud to call him a friend. The work he and Erin have done for Mississippi is remarkable. That bottle of bourbon Wright gave me still sits on the shelf behind me, unopened. It's a reminder of that year, of the struggle and the kindness that came with it.

When I got back home, I felt like I was starting over. Again. The crops were gone. The farm was underwater. The restaurant was managing, but barely. Once more, I was left to pick up the pieces. And yet, as I've learned time and again, there's always something good to hold onto. Even in the hardest years, there are moments of beauty. You just have to look for them.

CHAPTER 28

Replanting and Championships

What do you do in a scenario like this? That was the question I kept asking myself. Some of my fellow farmers talked about collecting insurance and walking away from the season. It made sense in a way. It was late in the year to be replanting soybeans, and any path forward was going to mean a significant loss of income.

But I'd run the numbers. I'd done my due diligence. No matter how I turned it over in my mind, one fact became painfully clear: there was no way I could pay the bills I had without putting some kind of crop in the ground, even as late as it was. Insurance wouldn't be enough. I had no choice but to replant. I would plant two crops in one year, but only harvest one.

It's one thing to make that decision. It's another to act on it, knowing you're working your butt off simply to limit your losses, rather than to make a profit. I was working hard for less than free.

Seed companies that had promised free seed in the event of replant were suddenly backpedaling on their commitments. Insurance money to buy seed was slow to arrive. There was a shortage of seed because the replant acreage was so vast. I had to scrape together whatever I could, going from one retailer to the next, taking whatever they had. It wasn't about what I wanted; it was about what I could get.

Each day, I fought through the old, dead soybean plants—knee-high and lifeless—to get the new seed in the ground. It was late June by then, and the land around my house told a very different story. My neighbors and good friends, the McCain brothers, grandsons of Mrs. Sullivan, farm the land adjacent to my home. The same land where I'd had my first job all those years ago, chopping cotton. It's higher ground and hadn't seen nearly the rain that drowned Shurden Farms. Their crops had survived—and not just survived, they were thriving. Each evening, I'd finish planting and come home to see their soybeans waist-high, dark green, and full of promise.

There aren't adequate words to describe how that felt. I've always loathed jealousy, but there were moments I couldn't help but ask, "Why me?" Why was my land flooded while theirs stood tall? Why was I replanting in late June while their fields were flourishing? I hated those thoughts, and I scolded myself a little for having them. Even now, writing this, I feel guilty for feeling that way. But the truth is—it was hard. Watching their success while I fought for mere survival wasn't easy. But I kept moving.

One of the few reprieves during that time was listening to Mississippi State baseball on the radio. Bryce would bring me the daily meat and three from the restaurant, and I'd make the best of it with Mississippi State in the background. They were having an incredible run, and it looked like this could finally be their year. I'd promised myself long ago that if State ever made it to Omaha again, I wouldn't miss it. But there I was—alone and stuck on the farm—trying to salvage what was left of the farming season while my alma mater was having an epic baseball season.

The next best thing was sending Mary Stafford. She was at Mississippi State then, and knowing she was there in Omaha somehow made me feel like I was there too, in both name and spirit. She sent pictures and Snapchats, keeping me updated on everything happening. She took pictures with Dak Prescott and the country music singer, Hardy. I was so glad she got to experience that. It wasn't the same as being there, but seeing her have a good time helped.

On my birthday, June 30, 2021, Mississippi State won the national championship in baseball for the first time in school history. I'd listened to every game on the radio, but that night, I parked the tractor early and went home to watch the final innings on TV. When the last pitch was thrown and the Dawgs stormed the field in celebration, I felt a strange mix of emotions.

There was pride, of course—pride in the team, pride in the state, pride in witnessing history made. But there was also panic. The kind of panic that creeps in when the world moves on and you're still stuck in the literal mud and muck, fighting to save what feels unsalvageable. I sat there, the glow of the TV reflecting off the pecky cypress walls of my den, and wondered how I was going to keep going. Once again, life felt tragic.

The crops weren't just crops. They were my way forward—my second chance, my attempt to claw my way out of the floodwaters and back to something resembling stability. Watching the celebration in Omaha, I couldn't help but feel like I was running my own kind of race—one where the stakes weren't a trophy, but something far more personal: survival.

That night, I went to bed with the sound of cheers still echoing in my mind. Pride and panic intertwined, pushing me forward—because there was no other choice. There never is.

CHAPTER 29

Bootcamp

By the time the dust settled on the crop, we had survived. Record soybean prices buoyed our income just enough to pay the bills, though survival came with a bitter aftertaste. It was hard not to let my mind run the numbers. If the weather had cooperated—if we'd had just an average yield and the costs of a single planting—we would've come out far ahead. Instead, we took a six-figure loss. Survival, without victory.

The flood of 2021 had been a defining moment, but it wasn't the only challenge that year. The restaurant—my other livelihood—was floundering. After the flood and the grind of replanting, I'd taken my eye off the ball. And, as it always goes in business, that was my fault. As I've noted previously, problems in a business always trace back to the owner. I was so focused on getting the farm back on track that I hadn't noticed how badly the restaurant was slipping.

It started with the new chef. He was talented—brilliant, even—but his tenure was short. For reasons personal to him, he didn't stay long. That left a void I wasn't prepared to fill. I moved a promising, hardworking go-getter into the manager role. She gave it her all, but the truth was, we didn't see the culture or food of the business in the same way. That was on me. I hadn't done the work to communicate my vision or train her in what I wanted Stafford's Market to be. In that moment, I'm not sure I was capable of communicating the vision to anyone, or if I even had one. The result was a disjointed kitchen, mediocre food, and a team dynamic that was holding us back.

Our sales were down. Our meat and three offerings—the very cornerstone of our business—had become average at best. The food wasn't bad, but it wasn't the kind of food that made people rave about us or tell their friends. And average doesn't keep the doors open.

I remember one Friday in November in painful detail. It was playoff season, and we were feeding the local high school football team. The manager had set up a buffet for the players—a high-carb, high-protein spread to give them the fuel they needed for the game. I swung by to wish them good luck and take a quick look at the food. When I saw the buffet, my heart sank. The food wasn't what I wanted it to be. It wasn't what it should have been. It was so bad, in fact, I was embarrassed. These boys, their coaches, and their parents—they deserved better. And the fault was mine.

For years, I'd been traveling the South reviewing gas station food. Some of these places were absolutely nailing the kind of food I thought I was doing—comfort food. They were delivering something special, something memorable, something worth driving out of your way for. I couldn't shake the idea that if a gas station could do it, I had absolutely no excuse.

I've always been a believer in daily incremental growth—the idea that if you focus on improving just a little each day, those small changes eventually compound into something extraordinary. But incremental growth wasn't going to cut it this time. If I didn't make bold, immediate changes, 119 North Main would become just another small-town restaurant that couldn't make it. Everything was on the table. I was willing to cut it all if that's what it took to save the business.

The week after Christmas, I made the decision to close the restaurant temporarily. I locked the doors—and locked myself inside. I needed time to face the hard truth. I had to have an honest conversation with myself. That week became my personal boot camp for restaurant owners. I pored over everything: the menu, the kitchen operations, the team dynamics, the numbers. Nothing escaped scrutiny.

It was brutal. I looked at every failure, every missed opportunity, and I owned it. I thought about all the gas stations I'd visited—the ones that were killing it—and asked myself, *Why them and not us? What do they know that I don't?* I broke down the way we ran our kitchen, the way we designed our menu, the way we delivered food to customers. I realized we weren't just doing things wrong—we were playing the wrong game entirely.

That week was transformative. By the time I unlocked those doors again, I had a new vision for Stafford's Market. I was ready to take the leaps that would change everything—not just small, daily steps, but a quantum leap such as advocated by Price Pritchett. I didn't know it then, but what I discovered during that boot camp week would go on to rewrite the rules of how I ran a restaurant.

It didn't just save my business—it reshaped my life. The changes we made led to a transformation so dramatic that I was later invited to speak at industry events about menu development and operational excellence. Articles now regularly quote me as an expert in the field.

That week after Christmas was a turning point. It forced me to step back, reassess, and reimagine what Stafford's Market could be. What came next wasn't just survival. It was reinvention. And it all started with a hard conversation in an empty restaurant.

CHAPTER 30

The Line Doesn't Hold Itself

If you've never stood at the back of a restaurant during a slammed lunch rush, you don't know what organized chaos smells like. It's the heat of fry oil and fresh rolls, the rattle of pans, the bark of tickets, and the weight of thirty people trying to eat in twenty minutes flat. It's a symphony held together by duct tape, sweat, and—if you're lucky—a team that knows how to dance without stepping on each other's toes.

That's what I have at Stafford's: a real team. Not just a random group of people clocking in and out. I didn't fully realize it until a few years ago. I used to think I was just managing a restaurant. But now I know I was building something much more valuable than a menu—I was building a team that could do amazing things, even if I were across a rice field or reviewing gas station sushi off the tailgate of my truck.

There are three people who keep this place alive—and each one holds it together in a different way.

Angie is the glue. She's the one who keeps us between the ditches. She never calls it in. Never shows up halfway. She's the first one here most mornings and the last to complain. When I'm busy thinking about big-picture stuff, Angie's handling the parts that keep the wheels from falling off. She doesn't need a spotlight—she needs a place that works. And she makes it work every single day.

Netsha is the heart. She's our cook, and every plate she sends out carries something more than seasoning. She doesn't talk much about it, but she cares deeply about the food, the people, and whether everyone's taken care of. Her food tastes like somebody's mama is back there. Not because she follows a recipe, but because she cooks like she means it. That kind of care can't be taught. It has to be lived.

And then there's Bryce—my confidant. She started here when she was seventeen. Now she's twenty-eight, and she's the soul of the front of house. She knows what's happening with the staff, the customers, and probably the weather three days from now. She's one of the most charismatic people I've ever met. We joke that if a new customer walks in, Bryce will know their Social Security number before they leave. But it's not really a joke. She makes people feel seen. Heard. Known. A lot of folks don't come to Stafford's just to eat—they come to talk to Bryce.

And that kind of connection—being open, warm, attentive—comes with risk. People will walk in here having a bad day or a bad life, and they'll take it out on an innocent bystander.

I remember one afternoon when an angry customer came in, already steaming before she got to the counter. Something wasn't right with her order, and instead of saying it, she started lashing out at Bryce—loud, aggressive, and foul-mouthed. Bryce kept her cool, but she came and found me, and I could see the frustration behind her eyes. Not fear. Not even anger. Just that tired, wounded look good people get when they've been hit for no reason.

So I walked out front and said, as calmly as I could, "Give her her money back." Then I turned to the customer and said, "Thank you, but don't come back."

That was it. I wasn't looking for a scene. But I also wasn't going to let anyone tear down one of my people. You cannot build a team unless they know you've got their back, especially when they're in the right. I know the line, "The customer is always right," but I have not found this to be true. You cannot play this game without a team.

Other employees have come and gone. Some made a mark. Some didn't. That's the nature of the business. But these three? These are my people. And the magic is that they're greater than the sum of their parts. One holds the line, one stirs the soul, and one brings the light. It takes all three to make Stafford's what it is.

I don't often brag on myself, but I'll say this: I know how to build a team. Not just hire bodies, but actually build a culture. I've learned that you can't lead unless you've got something real to lead. You can't inspire people who don't trust each other. And you can't expect great service from folks who don't feel like they matter.

A lot of businesses are just groups of strangers who happen to wear the same shirt. But not here. Not anymore. At Stafford's, we know each other's rhythms. We laugh. We yell. We pull each other through the hard days. We show up again and again—not just for the paycheck, but because it means something.

The truth is, the customer might remember the fried chicken or the cobbler, but what they really come back for is the feeling. The connection. The way this place makes them feel like they belong. That doesn't come from a marketing strategy. That comes from the back of the house, from the heart of it.

PART IV

Lessons, Legacy, Mindset

CHAPTER 31

A New Vision—The Grandma Rule

"Without a vision, the people perish"
– Proverbs 29:18

Here's a cold, hard truth: life isn't that hard to understand. Neither is business, farming, or the restaurant industry. What's hard is committing. Knowledge is everywhere. You don't need to enroll in school to learn how to frame a house, fix a watch, or manage a budget the Harvard way. There's a YouTube video for all of it—or just about anything you could dream of. But knowledge isn't the problem. The problem is finding an aiming point and never wavering. Discipline. That's the hard part.

Over the years, I've read all the books, attended the boot camps, and hired the coaches. None of it was about knowledge. Not really. It was about creating action and putting myself in the mindset of discipline. The smartest people in the world fail all the time, while those less talented, less educated, and less prepared succeed. This happens because success isn't about raw intelligence. It's about focus. When I've been focused—when I've had a clear vision for what I wanted—there was no stopping me.

That personal boot camp I put myself through after Christmas wasn't just a turning point; it was a reckoning. Losing over and over again, seeing failure after failure, had put me in a mindset of determination. I was angry—in the most productive way possible. Sick and tired of being sick and tired. I was a bright light, scattered but ready to be focused through the right lens. That week, I found clarity. I found vision.

One of the people who has helped me over the years is Coach Michael Burt. He has a theory: your vehicle—the very business or job you are in—might not be capable of getting you where you want to go. Sometimes, you have to ditch the vehicle entirely. Other times, you overhaul it. Rebuild the engine. Reupholster the seats. Slap on a fresh coat of paint and only fill the tank with premium. That's what I was doing during that week. I didn't scrap Stafford's Market, but I completely reworked it.

It started with one question: *What do I want Stafford's to be?*

I thought about Mammy. I thought about the meals I ate in her kitchen, the way the food and the love intertwined so seamlessly. I thought about Mrs. Sullivan, the McCain brothers' grandmother, and how her restaurant in the 1980s provided more than just a meal—it was a refuge from the Mississippi heat, a place where you could taste something that felt like home.

And then I thought about what they'd think if they walked into 119 North Main today. Would they be proud? Would they recognize the food? Or would they see it for what it had become: a scattered, unfocused mess trying to be too many things to too many people?

Here's the trap restaurant owners fall into, especially in smaller markets: we try to please everyone. A customer asks for a quesadilla, so we add it to the menu. Someone suggests Chinese food for the Sunday buffet, and we say, "Why not?" What starts as a small, focused menu balloons into a bloated mess. Even management books encourage this, with rules like, "Never have an ingredient on your menu that isn't used in at least three dishes." That sounds smart—until you realize you're creating new menu items just to justify the inventory you already have.

I had lost the plot.

There's a special place in life and business that I call *the identity crossroads*. It's where three paths converge: love, mastery, and value. Most people only walk one or two of these paths. But when you find the intersection of all three, everything changes. You've found your identity. Your purpose.

Imagine walking a shaded path in the woods. This is the path of love. You enjoy it, but it's slow going. Eventually, another path converges with yours—mastery. The path widens and becomes easier to navigate because now you're not only enjoying it, you're good at it. Finally, the path merges with a paved road—value. This is where what you love and what you've mastered gain meaning and serve others. And there, at the intersection, is your car—the one you just rebuilt. Now you're ready to fly.

For me, all paths led back to one thing: the food Mammy cooked. We were good at it, when we focused. It made up seventy percent of our sales as just one line on the menu. That was the sign I'd been ignoring. This was our mission. This was our identity.

Some call it soul food. Others call it country cooking. I just call it *grandma food*. And I decided Stafford's would be the best grandma food restaurant in Mississippi. Anything outside of a meat and three would be complementary to our identity.

We call it the Grandma Rule. It's simple: treat every customer like they're your grandma. When a plate doesn't look right, we ask, "Would you send this to your grandma?" Would your grandma eat canned green beans, or would she make something better?

The Grandma Rule transformed our business.

That week, I rewrote the entire menu. I cut it back to five core items and ditched anything we couldn't make from scratch. I added a smashburger, a shrimp po' boy, and a chicken sandwich—all inspired by Mammy and my travels. She would've loved them.

I also had to make tough calls. I don't buy into the idea that a workplace is a family. A workplace is a team, and every team member has a role to play. Sometimes, good players are on the wrong team. Joe Burrow sat on the bench at Ohio State. But when he transferred to LSU, he won a national championship. Both teams were good—he just wasn't in the right place at the right time.

I had to let my manager go. She was hardworking and talented, but she didn't fit the identity we were building. It was a hard call—but the right one.

When I met with the staff to share the new vision, they caught the excitement immediately. The Grandma Rule wasn't just a slogan—it was a mission they believed in. Sales took off. Each month, we hit new highs. Tables filled with people I'd never seen before—even in a small town where I thought I knew everyone.

I should mention: in those first few weeks, my team rewrote a lot of the recipes I had created during that reboot week. Saying things like, "My grandma did it like this." And most of the time? Their versions became the standard. They understood the assignment. We were a team again.

A couple of years later, I reviewed NFA Burger in Dunwoody, Georgia. The owner, Billy Kramer, only had five items on the menu, and that fascinated me. I asked him for a quote for a speech I was giving in Las Vegas, and he said: "I'd rather do one thing perfectly than a lot of things imperfectly."

He's right.

If you're in this business, don't overcomplicate it. Find the thing you're best at, and do the damn thing. Stay in your lane. Build your menu and your business around what you love, what you've mastered, and what brings value to others. That's the magic of the identity crossroads.

For Stafford's, it's "grandma food." For you, it might be something else. But when you find your vision, sell your team on it, and commit to it—when you have even a small team that's all on the same mission—you can move mountains.

CHAPTER 32

Worst to First

The printers are running as I write this. Somewhere in Jackson, or Tupelo, or maybe some warehouse tucked beside a two-lane road, fresh ink is hitting warm paper. The latest issue of *Mississippi Magazine* is rolling off the line.

You probably haven't heard of it if you're from somewhere else. But down here, in our little corner of the world, it's the gospel. It's how we tell ourselves who we are—and who we aspire to be. It's the yearbook of the good stuff: our people, our stories, and our food.

And when that magazine lands on porches and convenience store racks and waiting room tables across the state—and hell, across the country—there will be two bold little lines of print that say more than a hundred online reviews ever could:

"Best Blue Plate in Mississippi"
"Best Fried Chicken in Mississippi"

And below both of those titles, in black and white, it'll say:

"Stafford's Market, 119 North Main, Drew, MS."

Read that again. Not Jackson. Not Oxford. Not Biloxi. Drew.

A town with no stoplight and more history than tax revenue. A place most folks only know from a passing glance on Highway 49—or from "Archie who?" if they know it at all. But for one brief, shining moment, we were the heartbeat of Southern food. The underdog. The miracle. The gold medalist standing on the tallest podium, fists raised high, chicken breader still on our aprons.

We were up against titans: Georgia Blue, with its polish, muscle, and multiple locations; and Primos, older than sliced bread and just as essential to Central Mississippi. Names whispered with reverence in kitchens and dining rooms across the state. And there we were, playing the role of the scrappy cousin in some forgotten Tennessee Williams play. The gravel-throated gospel singer at the polished choir concert. The moonshine in a world of imported wine. But we won. Not as a fluke. Not as an afterthought. We won outright. No honorable mentions here. No footnotes. No asterisks.

That kind of thing makes you pause. Makes you go sit on the back steps after close, light a cigar—even if you don't smoke—and stare out at the flat fields that raised you. You think about all the burnouts and busts, the Tuesday lunch rushes that never came, the fryers that wouldn't stay lit, and the customers who never came back.

And then you think about obedience.

It's not a word we use much anymore. Sounds too much like giving up. Like giving in. But obedience to the process? That's different. That's sacred.

People talk about discipline like it's the peak. Like it's the mountain. But Christ didn't ask for disciplined followers. He asked for obedient ones. It's not the same. Discipline, while very important, is self-directed. Obedience is surrender. It's giving yourself wholly over to the mission, to the recipe, to the plate. Obedience is about trust that if you show up every morning, hungover or heartbroken, late on bills or short on staff, something will happen. The grease will get hot. The chicken will sizzle. The people will come.

And in a meat and three, that means focusing on the center of the plate—until it's so good, you don't have to shout about it. The sides? They'll come. They'll evolve. But the main thing? That's the gospel. That's the scripture. That's where your soul goes.

We didn't win because I'm clever, though God knows I can work a room, work social media, and shake the right hands. But handshakes don't get you this far. Not without the hours. Not without the obedience. Not without the days we showed up and cooked like it was Sunday supper for every soul we've ever loved.

From worst to first. From forgotten to undeniable. From Drew to the world.

CHAPTER 33

Ancestors or Ghosts

"Walk with the wise and become wise, for a companion of fools suffers harm." — Proverbs 13:20

I didn't get here on my own. Nobody does. We like to talk about self-made men in this country, but the truth is, all of us are shaped by the voices that speak into our lives—whether loud or quiet, early or late, harsh or kind. Sometimes they're teachers. Sometimes they're family. Sometimes they're just someone who showed up at the right moment and saw something in you that you hadn't yet seen in yourself. As Tennyson said, "We are a part of all that we have met."

My friend, Wright Thompson, once told me that we strive to be ancestors, not ghosts. We want to be people who are worthy of being lived up to, not just memories that drag others down. I definitely have ancestors.

For me, it started with Mammy. She didn't preach—she cooked. She didn't give big speeches about God or grit or grace. She handed you a plate and looked you in the eye. And somehow, that was enough. Her kitchen was my first classroom. I learned early that food is more than calories—it's communication and care. When she put fried chicken and freshly shelled butter beans with a square of cornbread on the table, it wasn't just lunch. It was her love language. I see you. You matter. Come sit down and rest a minute.

And then there was my dad. If Mammy taught me how to serve, he taught me how to stand. He didn't talk much either, at least not the way other men did. But I watched him: in the fields, in the courtroom, in the way he carried the weight of responsibility with quiet strength. He wasn't the loudest voice in the room, but he was consistent. Present. Obedient to the work in front of him. To the people who counted on him. That's a word I keep coming back to—obedience. It's not submission. Or maybe it is—submission to God, to the mission. It's resolve. It's the decision to stay the course when you'd rather turn around. It's service to others.

My dad's voice still echoes in my head when I'm tempted to take the easy way out—when I don't feel like getting up early or writing one more check or fighting for the thing I said I'd build. He never needed a pulpit. His life was the sermon.

There were others, too. Michael Burt came along when I needed a different kind of fuel. He reminded me that ambition isn't something to apologize for. That you can love your people and still want to win. That obedience to a vision isn't boring—in fact, it's holy. I started listening to guys like Jim Rohn and Tony Robbins, men who spoke a language that mixed business with faith and mindset with action. Their voices helped me name what I'd already learned in the Delta: success doesn't come from talent—it comes from showing up with purpose, every single day.

And then there's Leslie, my wife. No one has shaped me more. If Mammy's food healed me and my dad's example steadied me, Leslie's love carried me. Through the lean years, the long hours, the babies, bills, and busted equipment, she never wavered. I think maybe she was as hardheaded as me. She believed in me, and that helped me believe in myself. Her voice wasn't loud either. But it was constant. Like water carving rock. Like a hymn you hum without even realizing it—stuck in the back of your mind, always. Never gone.

When I think about the man I am today, I know exactly how I got here. It wasn't by force. It was by connection—by letting myself be shaped by the people who showed up, stood firm, stayed kind, and told the truth even when it was hard. I've learned that the loudest voices aren't always the most important ones. Sometimes, the most powerful things you'll ever hear come through a plate of food, a quiet hand on your back, or a look that says, "Keep going."

These are the voices that shaped me. And now—with this book, with my work, with my table—I try to return the favor.

CHAPTER 34

The Meet and Three Philosophy

In the South, we know a meat and three plate is how you build a meal—one main thing and three sides that hold it up. What I've learned is that life works the same way. But it's not just about the food. It's about who you meet along the way—yourself, your people, your work, and the world. This is my *meet* and three for life.

Everyone has a gift—sometimes given at birth, sometimes earned through fire. Through writing this, I've come to realize that my gift is connection. I do it better than most. All the farming, the cooking, and the hard days spent standing in judgment of my fellow man have honed that gift into something I use every single day. And it's been the single biggest contributor to any success I've ever had. When I look back, everything good in my life—every door opened, every hand shaken, every path made a little clearer—started with connection.

In the Delta, we measure life in meals. And like any great Southern meal, a life worth living has to have balance—a center of the plate that holds it all together, sides that bring flavor and strength, and something sweet to remind you why you sat down in the first place.

I didn't always know that. As a kid, I thought I was just chopping cotton, sweating through my shirt in the July sun, trying to earn a few dollars. But looking back, I see it more clearly: those fields taught me about grit. About finishing the row. About showing up when it's hard and sticking with it when it's boring. I learned it in the way Mammy would slide a plate across the table after I mowed her yard—not asking for thanks, just trusting I'd taste the lesson she was trying to teach. That food could heal. That quiet service could change your life. And I saw it in my father, who walked the rows at dawn and handed down second chances in the courtroom without ever needing applause. He didn't preach—he lived it: obedience, grit, quiet strength.

So when I talk about rules for life, I'm not talking about just philosophy. I'm talking about the lessons I sweated into my skin and tasted in Mammy's cornbread. I'm talking about how to build a life that actually feeds you.

Here's my **Meet and Three** for life: one main thing, three essentials supporting it, and a little something sweet to bind it all together.

The Center of the Plate: Meet Yourself First

You are the center of your own plate. If you don't know your own story—if you don't connect deeply with yourself—nothing else matters. Mindset is everything. Identity is everything.

I wasn't born Stafford Shurden. I built him. I built him through fire and failure, through lonely nights and early mornings, through showing up when quitting would have been easier. And if I've learned anything, it's this: you have a contract with yourself. If you don't pick your story, the world will write one for you. And trust me—the world doesn't always write kindly.

Mindset isn't about being motivated. It's about being obedient to the version of you that you promised to become. The only thing we have complete control over is our own mindset.

Side One: Meet Your People

Who you surround yourself with matters. Your team, your family, your brain trust—these are the *whos* that help you build your life. Nobody great built anything alone. Find people who push you, love you, challenge you, and believe in your vision even when you forget it yourself. You don't need a crowd. You need a circle—a team. Choose wisely.

Side Two: Meet Your Product

What are you giving the world? What's the work of your hands? For me, it's literal: fried chicken, meat and three, plates full of comfort and belonging. But the deeper truth is this—your product, your offering, has to be an extension of your core values. It has to feel like you. If you're selling something you don't believe in, people will taste it. If you're building something you wouldn't put your own name on, people will see it. Meet your product every single day and ask: "Would I serve this to my own family?" If the answer's no, fix it. Find something the world values as much as you do, and you'll be rich in the things that truly matter.

Side Three: Meet the World

You can't live in a grain bin. At some point, you have to lift your head and connect outward—with your customers, your community, your audience. If you're in business, that's marketing. If you're in life, that's simple human connection. Either way, it's not about being slick. It's about being real. It's about telling your story in a way that invites people in. Marketing isn't selling—it's serving. It's saying: "Here's who I am. Here's what I believe. And if you see something of yourself in it, come on in."

The Sweet Finish: Be of Service

Every good Southern meal ends with something sweet. And the sweetest thing you can add to your life is service. If you're building just for yourself, you'll never be full. Service is the cobbler. The fried pie. The grace you didn't earn but got anyway. Buddy Manning told his son, Archie, "Just be a good guy." Jesus said, *"Do to others as you would have them do to you." (Luke 6:31, NIV).* Same wisdom, different voices. When you live to help others—not for applause, not for credit, but because it makes you more human—everything else falls into place. That's not a theory. That's a fact.

CHAPTER 35

The Road Home

This morning, I drove down A. W. Shurden Road, like I have a thousand mornings before. Still dark. Just me, the headlights, and the ghosts. My father's name on the green sign. My reflection in the window. Me—trying to measure up to a man who never let anything slide.

The fields were quiet, holding their breath.

I could almost hear the crunch of my boots on dirt as a boy, following behind my dad, asking questions more with my eyes than my mouth.

I could see Mammy in her kitchen, stirring pots with a rhythm that felt like prayer, sliding a plate across the table like she was handing you a little piece of your own story.

Everything I am now started back there.

With the food.

With the faith.

With the feeling that a plate could hold not just nourishment, but truth.

I turned down Reed Road and passed the cemetery where my father is buried.

I always slow down there.

Not because I have to—but because some places deserve reverence.

Because some men still live in the way their sons try to live right.

I ask myself often: *Would he be proud of what I'm building? Of who I've become?*

The building at 119 North Main came into view, dressed in its new navy coat.

For twenty years, it wore that tired green like an old work shirt.

Now it has a fresh face—staring back at me like a new chapter.

Not just for the business.

For me.

Meet and Three.

It started as a meal. Became a business. And somewhere along the way, without me even realizing it, it turned into a way of life.

A philosophy.

When Mammy slid those plates across the table, it wasn't just about the best way to fry a pork chop.

When my dad stood in those courtrooms, it wasn't just about justice.

Both of them, in their own way, were pointing me toward the same truth:

Know what matters. Serve it up with heart. Stay obedient to the calling.

That's what Meet and Three means to me now.

- The center of the plate is **meeting yourself**: knowing your story, owning your purpose, staying faithful to who you said you'd become.

- The first side is **meeting your people**: building your circle, your team, your family, the ones who push you and catch you and believe in you when you forget how.

- The second side is **meeting your product**: doing the work of your hands with pride, whether it's a plate of fried chicken, a field of cotton, or a dream you planted when nobody else saw it.

- The third side is **meeting the world**: telling your story, showing your work, not by selling it slick, but by living it real and offering it to others.

And like any true Southern meal, the whole thing has to end with something sweet:

Service.

The quiet grace of giving back.

The understanding that what you build isn't just for you.

This is how we live down here.

This is how I've tried to build—every business, every decision, every prayer over every plate.

You don't have to chase every shiny thing.

You just have to plate what matters—with faith, with family, with farming, with food.

The tie that binds.

It always has been.

CHAPTER 36

What It All Comes Down To

I didn't write this book because I had all the answers. I wrote it because I wanted to understand the path that brought me here, and maybe help someone else find their footing on theirs.

And now, as I look back over the chapters, the years, the miles, and meals, I see that the story wasn't just about farming, or food, or family. It was about something deeper.

It was about what holds it all together.

The tie that binds.

I've come to believe that **identity is chosen, not inherited**. I wasn't born Stafford Shurden—I built him. Out of early mornings and hard lessons, late-night doubt, and grit scraped from Delta mud. I built him with a shovel in one hand and a skillet in the other. That's what this place gave me: the chance to become who I was always meant to be.

Somewhere along the way, I learned that **obedience matters more than motivation**. You won't feel inspired every morning. Most days, it's just you, the silence, and the weight of responsibility. But obedience—sticking to your principles, doing the work anyway—that's what gets you across the finish line. That's how you build a life that holds up in the storm.

I learned **that connection is the real currency**. Not cash. Not titles. But the laughter across a lunch counter. The nod of a regular. The look on someone's face when they take a bite and, just for a moment, remember their grandmother's kitchen. I've seen whole worlds change over a plate of food. You don't forget that. You need people, and they need you.

I learned that **work is sacred**. Not just what you do, but how you do it. From the rows of cotton to the corners of a dishroom, work done with pride is a kind of prayer. My daddy showed me that. The Delta taught me that.

And this land—this Delta—it may be poor in money, but it's rich in meaning. **Place shapes purpose**. The heat, the heartache, the hope of this place—it carved something into me that no city ever could. It made me stay. It made me care.

And maybe that's the final lesson: that **legacy is made in bold moves, and in a thousand daily decisions**. In showing up. In making the plate right. In forgiving. In serving. In telling the truth, even when it costs you.

So that's it. That's the meet and three.

Not just a meal. Not just a menu. Not even just a business.

A life. Built with purpose and passion. Seasoned with stories. Served with love.

Thanks for sitting at the table with me.

APPENDIX

On the Road Again: Gas Station Tailgate Review (a.k.a. The Sweet Finish)

The thing about having a vision—one so clear you could etch it into glass—is that it makes everything else easier. Identity breeds standards, and standards breed systems. Before I knew it, we had built something that could function without me hovering over it every second of the day. My team wasn't working for me; they were working with me, shoulder to shoulder, fully bought into the mission we had created together. And that changed everything.

It freed me up to do what I do best. It gave me time to chase stories, to taste, to listen, and to learn—to be the kind of world-class marketer I had always known I could be. So, when the demands of farming weren't too heavy, I hit the road. Many of you probably bought this book for that very reason.

I started pushing further out from Mississippi, stretching my routes, going wherever the food and the people called me. I collaborated with the National Association of Convenience Stores down in South Louisiana, chasing boudin and cracklins in places where the air itself tasted like smoked paprika and rendered pork fat. Taking some bags and Mary

Stafford, I drove 1,100 miles to the southernmost point in the US—only to get hit by a car while filming a review. Nothing says "commitment to the bit" like a rocking camera in Key West while it's still rolling.

I brought Anna Walton to the Meat Church of Kansas City—a temple of brisket and burnt ends where smoke clings to your clothes like a ghost that never wants to leave. I found Korean food in a gas station in Charleston, and bánh mì in New Orleans that tasted like the Vietnamese Quarter had been airlifted straight from Saigon—with a Southern twist. I was everywhere, and every mile I logged made me better at running my restaurant.

Because here's the thing: great food doesn't just happen. It's not an accident. There's a structure to it—a philosophy. The best places, whether they're in a white-tablecloth dining room or tucked inside a dusty, sun-faded Exxon, understand that culture, identity, and procedure matter just as much as ingredients. Every trip was a seminar, every meal a masterclass. I stole ideas shamelessly, tucked them away, and brought them home to refine.

And the food. The food. I've filmed over two hundred reviews now—not even counting the ones so bad I couldn't bring myself to upload them. Every one that made the cut had something good: a spice blend, a technique, a weirdly perfect ratio of fat to crunch to acid. But then there were the special ones—the ones that haunt me in the best way possible. The ones that pop into my head at random moments, making me crave something a thousand miles away.

Some places just have it. The right food, the right people, the right energy—the kind of magic that sticks to your ribs and your soul long after you've left. These are the places I can't stop thinking about. In the end, I think it's largely about culture. It's about how a place makes you feel, not just what it feeds you.

So here it is, the appendix that fans of the review will be crushed if I don't include: in no particular order, the twelve gas stations you *must* eat at before you die. Yeah, it's a little dramatic—but it's also completely accurate. These are the best of the best. These are the ones that changed the way I think about gas station food—and food in general.

I implore you, weary traveler: if you ever find yourself near one of them, do yourself a favor. Pull over. Order big. Soak in the culture of these places. They may not be around forever.

Oark General Store, Oark, AR (Episode 151)

Deep in the heart of the Ozark Mountains lies a hidden gem with an unassuming name: the Oark General Store. This isn't just any old store—Oark is the oldest operating store in Arkansas. Today, it has evolved into more of a restaurant and gas station than a traditional general store, and that's part of its enduring charm. The new owners recognized the steady stream of motorcycle and car enthusiasts winding through the Ozarks and knew these travelers needed a place to stop, refuel, and savor a good meal.

In a town of just 148 people, the Oark General Store has become a true community hub. At lunchtime, the place hums with activity, often spilling out into the outdoor pavilion. It's here, beneath the vast Arkansas sky, that you can enjoy their epic burger and hand-cut fries while the mountain breeze kisses your skin. The food is good—the kind of meal that makes you pause and appreciate the simple pleasures in life.

The Oark General Store has mastered the art of blending the old with the new. The rustic décor honors its storied past, with wooden beams, weathered boards, and vintage signs that whisper tales of yesteryear. Yet it seamlessly integrates modern comforts, creating a warm and inviting atmosphere where history and hospitality converge. It's fun to imagine that, a hundred years ago, a weary traveler might have gazed up at the very same ceiling and walls.

From their legendary burgers to homemade pies, every bite tells a story. The ingredients are fresh, the recipes time-tested, and the execution flawless. This place doesn't just feed you—it nourishes your spirit.

If you ever find yourself in the Ozarks, make a detour to Oark. It's not just a gas station stop; it's an experience. Your cellphone probably won't work in this remote outpost—and that's part of the charm. It's the kind of place that stays with you long after you've left, echoing in your memory like the call of the mountains themselves, as the stress of the day melts away.

Get the burger—thick, juicy, and grilled to perfection—and for the sake of all that is holy, get the fresh-cut fries. Golden, crispy, and just the right amount of salty, they're the kind of fries that make you wonder why you ever settled for anything less. If the weather's on your side, take your plate outside. Sit back, look at the mountains, and let the breeze carry your troubles away. And if you're not full? Go back in for pie.

Joe's Kansas City Bar-B-Que, Kansas City (Episode 150)

Joe's Kansas City Bar-B-Que is the high temple of BBQ in the meat Mecca of BBQ towns. It stands as a testament to the transformative power of exceptional food served in the most unassuming of places. Housed in a working gas station on the corner of Forty-Seventh and Mission, Joe's defies expectations and rewrites the rules of what a gas station can be. This isn't just a barbecue joint—it's the destination of a pilgrimage for those in search of smoked meat nirvana.

I don't have to tell you this place is good. Everyone already knows. Anthony Bourdain listed Joe's in his article, "Thirteen Places to Eat Before You Die." That piece inspired this section of the book. Many, including Bourdain, believe the best BBQ in Kansas City is tucked away in this humble gas station.

Founded in 1996 by Jeff and Joy Stehney, Joe's began with a simple yet ambitious goal: to bring championship-quality barbecue to the masses. The Stehneys transformed this modest location into a world-renowned destination, drawing from Kansas City's rich BBQ tradition and infusing it with their own signature style.

The secret to Joe's success lies in its uncompromising commitment to quality. The Z-Man sandwich—a decadent stack of brisket, provolone cheese, onion rings, and barbecue sauce—is a masterclass in balance and indulgence. This is not fast food. It's slow food done right, each bite a testament to hours of patient smoking and craftsmanship that borders on obsession.

Walking into Joe's, you're immediately struck by the juxtaposition of the ordinary and the extraordinary. The gas station setting is permeated by the intoxicating aroma of smoked meat, and a line of eager patrons—locals and out-of-towners alike—winds through the space. It's where the gritty reality of a roadside pit stop meets the soulful artistry of true barbecue, creating an atmosphere as singular as the food is unforgettable. This place is a culinary landmark.

Get the Z-Man. And if you're lucky—if they haven't already sold out—treat yourself to the burnt ends. Those smoky, caramelized nuggets of pure barbecue bliss are meat candy you'll never want to stop eating.

Kent & Sue's Quick Stop, Bay St. Louis, MS (Episode 77)

Nestled on the far edge of Bay St. Louis, Mississippi, Kent & Sue's Quick Stop is an unassuming gas station that has garnered a loyal following for its exceptional seafood, especially my favorite, the shrimp po' boy, a sandwich I once used as the benchmark for my own version at Stafford's.

Far from your typical roadside stop, this place has become a local legend, thanks to the unwavering dedication of the owners. Their commitment to quality food and warm service has transformed what could have been just another convenience stop into a beloved community staple.

Kent & Sue's offers a menu that reads like a love letter to the Gulf Coast. Their biscuits and gravy are the stuff of local lore, drawing in daily visitors who swear by their homey goodness. The crawfish, a regional delicacy, is another standout—prepared with a flair that keeps patrons coming back for more.

But it's not just the food that makes this place special. It's the welcoming atmosphere, like stepping into a friend's kitchen. Regulars are treated like family, and newcomers quickly feel at home, often receiving impromptu tutorials on the finer points of Southern cuisine, like the proper way to eat crawfish.

Be prepared. You'll notice a hint of Louisiana in the accents at Kent & Sue's, which pairs beautifully with the smell of boiled seafood drifting through the parking lot. Get the shrimp po' boy. The bread is unbelievably fresh, and they make their own tartar sauce. You'll need it to dip the shrimp that tumble off this overstuffed work of art.

Delicias Bakery, West Palm Beach, FL (Episode 113)

On a trip to Florida, I stumbled across Delicias—and let me tell you, the best sandwich I had on that entire trip came from here. I wish I could tell you what it was called, the name escaped me even then, but it was a culinary masterpiece.

Tucked away like a secret in the heart of Florida, Delicias Bakery has been a cornerstone of its community since opening in May 2003. This hidden gem churns out hot, fresh Cuban bakery specialties that'll make you wonder why you ever settled for anything less.

The air is thick with the rich aroma of café con leche and cortaditos, drawing you in with an irresistible allure. Their steak sandwiches and pastelitos bring the flavor of Cuba to Florida.

Delicias isn't just serving pastries and sandwiches; they're dishing out slices of Cuban soul, one bite at a time. This place is for locals. The culture isn't a shock—it's part of the charm. It's where tradition meets taste. And if you speak Spanish, all the better.

And for the love of God, get the flan cheesecake. Trust me—it's a slice of heaven that will haunt your taste buds in the best possible way.

Vautrot's, Church Point, LA (Episode 144)

Down in the heart of Acadiana, life moves to a different rhythm. Around here, every gas station seems to double as a meat market and a full-fledged restaurant. Sure, the big names—Best Stop and Billy's Boudin—get plenty of love (and they deserve it). But me? I'm drawn to the smaller mom-and-pop places. If you find yourself in Church Point, make your way to Vautrot's (pronounced Votros), where owner Josh Venable runs the show with a dedication as fierce as a Louisiana swamp.

Vautrot's isn't just another stop on the road—it's a culinary sanctuary. Josh keeps his ingredients fresh and his standards high. Every dish that leaves the kitchen reflects his deep commitment to quality. Yes, everything here is good—but the boudin? It's world-class. Josh uses only fresh herbs, never dried ones like the big stores do. Sure, that means a shorter shelf life—but it's irrelevant. His boudin flies off the shelves faster than he can make it.

Vautrot's isn't just about the boudin. It also serves up killer meat and three lunches, crafted with time and passion, honoring the old ways. These meals aren't just thrown together—they're lovingly prepared, a tribute to the traditions that make Acadiana's cuisine so special.

In a world where convenience often trumps quality, Vautrot's is a breath of fresh, herb-infused air. It's a place where the pace is a little slower, the food a little richer, and the experience a lot more memorable. Josh Venable has created something truly special—a place where the spirit of Acadiana comes alive in every bite. If you're ever passing through, make it a point to experience Vautrot's.

Get the boudin. Because if you're in this part of Louisiana and you don't, what are you even doing? Smoky, rich, and packed with just the right balance of spice and fat—plus those fresh greens—it's the kind of boudin that reminds you why this dish is a religion down here. Then, get the meat and three. Whatever's on the menu that day, you can't go wrong—even if you've never heard of it. They'll call it "stew," and it'll be brown and served with rice. Just trust me. This is Cajun comfort food at its best. You'll wonder why you don't live closer.

Vine Brothers, Centreville, MS (Episode 93)

Benny Vine is the third generation to helm this storied establishment, and his passion for the craft is palpable. What started as a humble smokehouse turning out sausage and bacon for the small community of Centreville has, under Benny's stewardship, transformed into a full-fledged culinary destination.

Years ago, Benny expanded, moving into a gas station and growing his small smokehouse into a full-service meat market that now sets the standard. Not one to stop there, he added a restaurant and catering service, specializing in meals for surrounding industries. Benny's eyes light up when he talks about food—each dish steeped in south Mississippi green hickory smoke and the rich tradition of the Vine family legacy.

Walking into Vine Brothers, you can feel the history. The aroma of smoked meats is a siren call, pulling you into a world where time slows down and the food demands your full attention. The market is a carnivore's dream, showcasing cuts of meat that reflect Benny's unwavering commitment to quality.

But it's not just about the meat. Vine Brothers processes deer harvested by hunters from both Louisiana and Mississippi, adding another layer to its offerings. Benny has a knack for discovering new income streams that fit perfectly with what he's already doing—a mark of a savvy businessman who knows his roots and how to grow them.

The restaurant is a revelation. Whether you're grabbing a quick bite or sitting down for a full meal, the flavors are deep, smoky, and unforgettable. The catering service has become a lifeline for local industries, delivering hearty, delicious meals that keep workers fueled and satisfied.

This is one of those out-of-the-way places that you can't wait to return to. Vine Brothers isn't just a store—it's a testament to what happens when tradition meets innovation. Benny Vine has created a space where history and modernity coexist, and where every bite is a tribute to the generations that came before.

If you find yourself in Centreville, make a beeline for Vine Brothers. It's a journey into the heart of smokehouse tradition, with a taste that lingers long after you've left.

Go all in on the full buffet, and whatever you do, don't skip the smoked pork chops. You'll leave stuffed—maybe even regretting that last bite, if only for a second. And before you roll out, grab some Vine Brothers smoked sausage for the road. Toss it in the cooler, take it home, and fire up the grill.

Fratesi's Grocery, Leland, MS (Episode 51)

Nestled in the small town of Leland, Mississippi, Fratesi's Grocery is a living testament to the rich tapestry of immigrant history that defines the

Mississippi Delta, my home. The story of Fratesi's is deeply intertwined with the Italian families who journeyed to America in the early twentieth century, landing in New Orleans and making their way north to the fertile lands of the Delta.

The Fratesi family, like many other Italian immigrants, came seeking new opportunities and a fresh start. They brought with them not only a spirit of hard work and determination, but also their culinary traditions and a deep love for community. This blend of Italian heritage and Southern hospitality has been the backbone of Fratesi's Grocery since day one.

Walking into Fratesi's is like stepping back in time. The store exudes history—vintage décor, a warm, inviting atmosphere, and a sense of continuity carefully preserved through generations. Fratesi's has grown into a cherished local institution, adapting to changing times while staying true to its roots.

There's a big-city energy in the restaurant. Orders are shouted back to the kitchen with a kind of organized chaos. The menu? A beautiful blend of Italian favorites and Southern classics. They serve the local farming community because they themselves are farmers. It's a whole different vibe when the Delta sun starts to hang low and the old men file in to share an evening beer. This is one of those places you won't soon forget.

Order anything here, and you won't be disappointed. Clichéd as it sounds, it's the truth. The meat and three is always a solid bet, but the locals swear by the cheesesteak, and for good reason. And while I'm nowhere near a vegetarian, I've got to admit: there's something about the fried olive po' boy—salty, briny, and completely unexpected—that keeps pulling me back.

Dodge's Store, Multiple Locations (Episode 108)

When it comes to the "hot box" game, few do it as well as Dodge's Store. And yeah, I might be a bit biased—the owner's wife hails from my tiny hometown of Drew. But bias aside, their reputation speaks for itself. The food is always hot, fresh, and the box is perpetually full. Whether you're grabbing a bite for breakfast or chasing down a midday craving, Dodge's delivers every time.

Their breakfast biscuits are fluffy, buttery, and just the right amount of crispy around the edges. But the real showstopper is their chicken on a stick. Picture this: a bamboo skewer loaded with marinated chicken, potatoes, onions, and pickles—all battered and deep-fried to golden perfection. It's a symphony of flavors and textures that might just be the best version I've had anywhere. They call it a chicken kabob. But it's my book, so they're wrong—chicken on a stick!

Dodge's isn't just resting on its laurels. They're rolling out new stores with bathrooms that rival Buc-ee's and drive-throughs designed for today's fast-paced world. These aren't just places to gas up—they're hot food destinations.

Get the chicken on a stick. The chicken is marinated overnight, soaking up every bit of flavor before getting battered and fried to golden perfection in peanut oil. The trick? Get a little of everything in each bite—the tang of the pickle, the sweet onion, the starchy fried potato, and that impossibly juicy chicken. There's plenty of good food here, but this is the move. Nothing else even comes close.

Mt. Herman General Store, Mt. Herman, LA (Episode 99)

Sure, places like Middendorf's Fish House, just off I-55, have gotten their due—their paper-thin fried catfish now a Louisiana institution. But across the state, there are countless gas stations and small restaurants holding it down—feeding the mechanics, the farmers, and the old-timers who come in for coffee and stay half the day. Mt. Hermon General Store is one of those places.

You wouldn't give it a second glance driving by—just a worn metal building. I missed it the first time, and I was trying to get there. But step inside, and it all starts to make sense. They've got the old movable-type Coca-Cola menu board—a signal they've been around a while; a quiet message of good food that cuts through the constant hum of a decades-old cooler.

Let me make this simple: You come here for the fried chicken with rice dressing. When I posted the original video, it was controversial. Many Louisianans came for me for calling dirty rice "rice dressing." I don't know what to tell you. In Mt. Hermon, they call it rice dressing.

Whatever the name, the chicken is everything fried chicken should be. Perfectly crisp, deeply seasoned, with skin that crunches just right before giving way to impossibly juicy meat. Call the side whatever you want—but it's the best I've ever had. Deeply seasoned, packed with some voodoo mix of spices that just works, and finished with just the right hit of green onion to bring it all together. And while you're at it, get one of those fried rolls, because why wouldn't you take an already perfect piece of bread and dunk it in hot oil?

Slovacek's and Czech Stop, West, Texas (Episode 83)

On September 15, 1896, William Crush had a wild idea: promote the new railroad by staging a head-on train collision just outside the city of West, Texas. The event drew 40,000 spectators to what was temporarily called "Crush, Texas." When the two locomotives smashed into each other at full speed, their boilers exploded, sending metal shrapnel flying into the crowd. Hundreds were injured. At least three people were killed. What was supposed to be a spectacle turned into chaos, forever branding the event in Texas history as "The Crash at Crush."

Just a few miles from that infamous site, another battle for dominance is underway. But this time, instead of colliding locomotives, it's a war of kolaches between two legendary gas stations.

On one side of Interstate 35 sits Czech Stop, a Texas institution that's been satisfying travelers for decades. Just across the highway stands the modern, well-equipped Slovacek's. Both serve up incredible kolaches, and both fiercely defend their claim to be the best in West.

West, Texas, is the heart of the state's Czech community. Czech immigrants began arriving in the mid-1800s, drawn by the promise of fertile land and economic opportunity. By the late nineteenth century, thousands had settled in central Texas, bringing their language, customs, and—most importantly—their food.

One of their most beloved contributions is the kolache. Originally a sweet, fruit-filled pastry from central Europe, kolaches were traditionally made for special occasions. But when the Czechs put down roots in Texas, their culinary traditions evolved. That's how the klobasnek was born—a savory version of the kolache, stuffed with sausage, cheese, and sometimes jalapeños.

Today, the word "kolaches" covers both sweet and savory varieties. They're as much a part of Texas now as brisket or Tex-Mex.

Which is better—Czech Stop or Slovacek's? That depends on who you ask. Die-hard traditionalists might swear by Czech Stop. Others love the variety and modern experience at Slovacek's.

Me? I lean toward the sausage-stuffed kolache at Slovacek's. There's just something about biting into that warm, pillowy dough and getting a rush of meaty, peppery flavor that feels like Texas itself.

One thing's for sure: this battle has no losers, only a long line of satisfied customers. Try both. Then let me know what you think.

Chevron, Satsuma, AL (Episode 136)

In Alabama, there's a sausage with a following that borders on religion. Conecuh isn't just a brand—it's a way of life. You'll find it sizzling at both Auburn and Alabama tailgates, a rare unifier in a state where loyalties don't waver. I know some good ol' boys over there who would throw hands over Conecuh's rightful place at the top. I use it here in Mississippi, and let me tell you—it's damn good.

You see Conecuh everywhere—on backyard grills, in gas station biscuits—but there's just something about eating it within a hundred miles of Evergreen, Alabama, where it's made.

If you ever find yourself rolling down I-65 in South Alabama, take the Satsuma exit and look for a plain old Chevron station. Locals just call it the Satsuma Chevron, but what they don't tell you is that it's world famous for something called *breakfast gumbo*.

Now let's be clear: I'm a gumbo purist, and this ain't gumbo in any traditional sense. It's more like a breakfast bowl—a glorious mess of grits, cheese, eggs, green onions, and of course, Conecuh sausage.

Don't play shy—you have to ask for it. I didn't see it on any menu board. Just say, "Breakfast gumbo, please," and when they ask if you want hot sauce—for the love of the Almighty, say yes. That little kick of heat and tang of vinegar takes it to another level.

The Original Brown Derby, New Orleans, LA (Episode 169)

I love New Orleans. Every time I go, I fall for it a little more. The city is a true melting pot, where cultures don't just blend—they stand side by side. And then there's the food. No place in the world tempts me to eat like New Orleans. That includes gas station food, which, like everything else here, is on another level. There's the ever-present Brother's chain, serving up fried chicken that feels like a cousin to Popeye's. Key's Fuel Mart, just outside the French Quarter, might have some of the best fried chicken in any city, period. Dan's, with locations all over, turns out solid po' boys. Don't forget Banh Mi Boys, serving up traditional bánh mìs with a distinct New Orleans twist.

But my favorite? The legendary Original Brown Derby. Now, I have to be honest: Brown Derby lost its gas pumps a few years back. But it still earns a place on my list because it's that damn cool. The food is great, but the vibe is what pulls me in. Ken, the owner, posts up by the front door, sitting on a five-gallon bucket, greeting every customer with that unmistakable New Orleans drawl: "You da best," he says—and somehow, you believe him. The place serves real-deal New Orleans soul food: neckbones, fried chicken, greens, pork chops, mac and cheese, and more. No other spot in the city offers a bigger selection at lunch, and according to Ken, no one else cooks like they do anyway.

When you walk out with a plate so heavy it bends the Styrofoam, you already know you made the right choice. Trust me on this one. It's the opposite of a tourist trap, and you'll be back.

The Traveler

"Travel is fatal to prejudice, bigotry, and narrow-mindedness, and many of our people need it sorely on these accounts. Broad, wholesome, charitable views of men and things cannot be acquired by vegetating in one little corner of the earth all one's lifetime." — Mark Twain

When I first started *Gas Station Tailgate Review*, it was nothing more than an advertisement for Stafford's—a way to put my name and my food in front of more people. But something happened along the way. Somewhere between a gas station burger in Georgia and a fried pork chop sandwich in Louisiana, it stopped being just marketing and became something else. A school. A church. A never-ending lesson in food, people, and the small, beautiful differences that make a place a place.

I travel, and I learn. Every stop, every gas station, every meal changes me a little. Our smash burger is a copy of NFA in Georgia, our shrimp po' boy stolen from Kent & Sue's in Bay St. Louis. I've picked up recipes and techniques like souvenirs—not just adding them to my menu, but to the way I see the world. I've even stopped to talk to farmers in the sugarcane fields of South Louisiana. No part of my life has gone untouched.

But it's not just about the food and the farming. It's the rhythm of these places—the way people talk, what they care about. I've driven through towns like Algoma, Mississippi; Bessemer, Alabama; and Seewee, South Carolina—places that wouldn't make most people's itineraries. But those places have taught me things. They've made me wiser.

Mississippi alone is proof that food and people shift in subtle but undeniable ways. The northeast clings to the culture of Appalachia, while the Gulf Coast carries the laid-back ease of a beach town, filled with Vietnamese influences and seafood shacks. East Mississippi holds onto the old South—the good parts, anyway—and the Delta, my home, feels like another country entirely. A place where history and hardship and the soul of the blues seep into everything, even the food.

Mark Twain was right. He wrote those words because his travels forced him to confront his own prejudices. And I think if we're honest, we all have our own. I know I did. But getting out of my little corner of the earth and breaking bread with strangers has been the best cure for all of it. Eating the food of a place tells you something about its people—about what they've been through and where they're headed. And when you share a meal with someone—really sit down with them—walls come down.

So hit the road. Find a place you've never been. Eat something that feels unfamiliar. Maybe from a gas station. You'll come back different and—if you do it right—better.

THANK YOU FOR READING MY BOOK!

Just to say thanks for buying and reading my book, I would like to connect with you and invite you to be a part of my circle!

Scan the QR Code:

I appreciate your interest in my book and value your feedback, as it helps me improve future versions. I would appreciate it if you could leave your invaluable review on Amazon.com with your feedback. Thank you!

www.ingramcontent.com/pod-product-compliance
Lightning Source LLC
Chambersburg PA
CBHW030248010526
44107CB00031B/1358/J